M... any-thing remarkable the way all his ... and sisters did. There were two clever ones above him and two clever ones below; it was like being the only common striped tabby in a family of splendid Persian cats. He hadn't even got a special friend, someone to whom he really mattered. Most of all, he wanted to impress his brilliant father, but nowadays he hardly seemed able to speak to him at all.

Then Midway the wonderful tiger came along. He was better than any friend any of the others had ever had. You could say that Midway existed only in Mark's mind, but with his help Mark began to feel like the interesting, independent sort of person he had always wanted to be, and in the end he did something braver and more wonderful than anything his elder brother Sebastian had *ever* done.

A good book for everyone with imagination, especially lonely people.

Cover design by Peter Whiteman

ANNE BARRETT

Midway

Illustrated by Margery Gill

Penguin Books

Penguin Books Ltd, Harmondsworth, Middlesex, England
Penguin Books Australia Ltd, Ringwood, Victoria, Australia

—

First published by Collins 1967
Published in Puffin Books 1971

—

—

Made and printed in Great Britain
by Richard Clay (The Chaucer Press) Ltd,
Bungay, Suffolk
Set in Monotype Juliana

I

THE splendid dream, in which Mark was galloping a horse through the sky, suddenly stopped. The strands of mane between his fingers changed into sheet and instead of round, warm flanks his legs could only feel each other down the bed. As if the horse had sat down abruptly and slid him off on to the blue-gold seashore where they had been riding, he came down with a bump; then both Mark's mount and the sky-sand vanished. There was a last cry and flutter of white gulls rising and only two dingy old London pigeons, crooing away to each other on the window-sill, were left. From the clear and dazzling place where he had been Mark was back in his bedroom again.

It was pretty dazzling there too, actually, because the morning sun was coming in. After the third blink Mark's eyes stayed open and he stopped trying to get the dream horse back again. He watched the two pigeons drowsily. Then, as a third one dropped down beside them on the window-sill, he was suddenly completely awake. For like the new pigeon his daily hope had come swooping back to him. Could it have happened today? Could it really have happened at last?

Mark kicked off the bedclothes, and looked down at his legs. He felt his head and hair, blinked hard and did a trial sort of think. It was no good. He was exactly the same as yesterday. His spirits sank.

Day after day he hoped that when he woke something astonishing might have happened to him; that a miracle might have taken place overnight and he would find himself completely different. He hoped that his muscles might have grown enormous, or his thoughts become very startling; that he would wake up knowing he wanted to be something quite definite and original, like a violin player or a marine biologist, and leap eagerly out of bed and start studying for it there and then. That was what everyone seemed to expect of him; that was the sort of thing that Seb and Evie did.

But it hadn't happened. The legs touching the floor were the same old knobbly ones he was used to, the hair he rubbed still felt the rough, dusty stuff of yesterday. He pulled one hair out and looked at it in the sunlight, then let it fall disgustedly. Still mouse. As he blinked in the brightness he guessed that his eyes wouldn't have changed either; there

seemed small hope that they might have turned blue and piercing, like an explorer's, overnight. He certainly had no feelings that any super-flashing intelligence was coming out of them for his thoughts still seemed to be going along the same old tracks. What there was for breakfast and whether he had left time to eat enough of it ... where was his other sock ...

No: he was still his dull old self; ordinary as the pigeons on the window-sill, except that they could fly. Mark looked at them sourly; the gift seemed wasted on them.

With one toe he fished up the missing sock from under the bed and looked at the name tape disgustedly. He would have two M's in his name and it would have to be the letter in the middle of the alphabet – if he had been called Anatole or Zigismund things might have been better. But Mark! Mark Munday! Something that made you think of marking ink and form marks and straight upright lines, not to mention the dreariest day of the week. In the temporary darkness made by pulling his jersey over his head Mark brooded about the unfairness of his lot.

Munday. When it was added on to Max, making his father's name, it sounded splendid, and so it did with Seb. But then if you put Sebastian in front of any name, or Seb's face on top of it, it was bound to seem unusual. And as for Evie – well, if you hung a yard of bright, dark red hair on to it even a name like Smith would stand out.

As Mark pushed his head up through the opening of his jersey and brought down his semaphoring arms the first things he saw were the crumb-picking pigeons on the sill again. They were ordinary all right, slatey-grey with pink feet, like a million other London pigeons, but he didn't suppose they cared. Neither would he have minded if the rest of his family hadn't been so very un-ordinary and if they hadn't kept rubbing it in. Not on purpose, of course, but just by being surprised all the time, as though they could hardly believe that anyone belonging to them could think and say such obvious, footling things.

His sandals had gone even farther under the bed than his socks and the abrupt movement that he made when he came the right way up again after finding them frightened the pigeons away. S MUNDAY, said one of the shoes that was dangling from a finger, inside the heel, but the S had been crossed out and an M put underneath. Mark tried to think of Seb slopping about in them but he couldn't; it wasn't possible to think of the elegant Seb in his sort of clothes at all. He looked at the sandals, which his own feet had turned up cheerfully at the toes, and wondered if anyone would ever cross out the M and put an A. Then, as he blew off a bit of fluff, he shook his head. You couldn't think of Adam in anyone else's shoes any more than you could Seb. It was only he, old middle Mark, and born in March too, of course, who had to wear other people's things. His thoughts slid back into the same little ditch again and he felt sorry for himself.

Two clever ones above him and two clever ones below; it was like being the only common striped tabby in a family of splendid Persian cats. It seemed as though his parents had taken a rest from making clever children when it came to him.

'Ziss ...' Mark's spirits lifted a bit as he began to skate his hairbrush over his head, pretending he was planing wood, but the gloomy thoughts were still going on underneath. As he thought of his parents, particularly his father, he stopped planing and sighed.

His father was so splendid, and Mark adored him, but nowadays he hardly seemed able to speak to him at all. In the form room at school there was a large print of a lion, looking superb, noble and slightly worried, and that was how Mark saw his father, Max Munday. He was tall, broad and solid and had large, fine-looking eyes, the sort that statues had. They either gazed away into the distance when he was thinking, which made them look extra clever and extra blue, or, when his attention was on you, they fixed you with a look of such kindly interest that it was like having a tingling wire drawn tightly between you. His lion's hair was thinnish on top but thickened out into a tawny bush behind his ears and he had a way of padding quietly out of his study in his slippers and prowling up and down the passages between his patches of thinking and writing, when he was waiting for the next idea.

Mark's father was writing about a tremendously important discovery he had made about memory and the way people's minds worked, particularly children's, and everyone said that it was going to make him, and because of him, perhaps even England, very famous. Mark had heard talk about some very special international prize and just lately he knew that it had become very urgent and hurried for his father to get the work finished because this award was going to be made after a series of lectures had been given by him and various other people, in a few months' time.

Sometimes on his prowls Max Munday would stop and ask Seb or Evie a question and be very interested at their answers; he would look at them keenly, nod, and then go straight away and write it all down. It was Mark's dearest wish to say something that would give his father that look, make him nod his head and hurry back into the study, but it had never happened yet. In the beginning he had tried to say clever things but they always went wrong; his father, who always took everything his children said seriously, had tried to make something of them but only ended by looking puzzled and Mark had given it up.

But hope kept springing up from time to time; perhaps today he might think of something. Mark reckoned that his hair should be done by now and dropped the brush. To save Tata, who did everything in the Munday household, they were all supposed to make their own beds, so he pulled his up. The effect, over his hairbrush, pyjamas, and some books he had been reading was rather lumpy, and as he went on thinking about his father he tried to thump it out even.

There had been a time, he thought, dealing with the front edge, when he could remember the Lion sitting here beside his bed at night, telling him stories in that lovely rolling voice that could roar at the exciting parts, be richly ordinary in the middle and then quieten down to a seashell whisper. Mark could remember how comfortable it had felt to be lying there and listening to him, in the twilight, before the room grew dark. But that was before the twins were born, when he was still the youngest and most special one; when there had still been hope that he might come out unusual too, like Seb.

It seemed a long time ago and Mark remembered it like last year's summer holidays, full of sun. After Adam and Lucy were born everyone's attention went on to praising them and Mark had got left out in the middle, with no one to notice him. He had tried hard to get attention for a while, but it didn't work and the effort even made him stammer sometimes, so that people got more impatient with him than ever. When he started talking in his sleep as well they put him in a room of his own. Well, he thought, that was one good thing that had come out of it anyway.

He stood up from poking the bed-spread down the back of the bed and looked round. It was better than having to share with silly Adam, better than feeling stupid all the time with Seb. Lucy still slept with Tata, or their mother, when their mother was there.

Mrs Munday came from Hungary and she had Evie's bright hair and the same enormous dark eyes as the twins, which made them so much admired. But the thing you noticed most about her, apart from her accent, was the funny sort of husky voice she had, which was entirely her own. Her eyes, instead of being fixed in the twins' unwinking stare, darted about as much as her mind did and the family seldom had the slightest idea where she would be, or what she would be doing next. This suited Max Munday, who had to be much alone with his work anyway, and both he and the elder children enjoyed her unexpectedness and her bright, sudden, bird flights in and out of their lives. It was only Mark who had a feeling that mothers ought to stay put and be there at tea-time; it was just his dullness again, he supposed. For Mrs Munday disagreed violently with the idea of anyone ever being at the same place the same time every day just out of habit and because they thought they ought to, and this – until Tata took over – had caused a lot of confusion for poor Mark at school.

Mrs Munday was an artist. Sometimes she shut herself in her studio and painted and sometimes she went dashing off to give exhibitions: sometimes you would find her giving lessons to a lot of strange people at home, when there would be much more noise in the flat than usual and lots of unknown people wandering up and down the stairs. Sometimes she did neither, but would settle momentarily to re-decorate the sitting-room, run up bright dresses for Evie and Lucy and make fierce red-pepper stews. But whatever she did and wherever she did it she was always so full of energy that Mark thought of her like the little red line that ran perpetually round the electricity meter.

Seb and Evie adored her and Mark expected that he would too, when he grew up to her, but what he wanted at the moment was an ordinary mother to go to Speech Days, and by no stretch of the imagination could Mrs Munday be called that. She used to look at Mark in a puzzled sort of way.

'This is the middle one, my little English boy,' she would say when she introduced him to anyone, as if she found summed up in him all the peculiarities of her adopted English race.

No, it was Tata who held the family together. It was she who shopped, cooked, washed and did everything else for them and Mark could hear her banging about in the next door dining-room now. Tata, also Hungarian, was small and fat, and Seb always said that she must have grown circular from going round and round like a spinning top, while she looked after the family's needs. As the children used to tug at her skirt when they were small they pulled now at her mind with all their wants. Perpetually flustered, she was always starting off in one direction, clapping her hand over her mouth as she remembered something else she ought to be doing, turning round and setting off again, till she looked like a clockwork toy that had gone wrong. But she was so fiercely possessive about the family that she wouldn't let anyone else in to help her, and somehow most things got done in the end.

Unlikely as it seemed, she had once been a ballet dancer. One Christmas Mark had been taken to see the ballet at Covent Garden and more than even by the firebirds or the princes he had been fascinated by the thought that old Tata had once been one of those dancers. Ever afterwards he had a picture of her spinning round from one job to another all day and then at night, collapsing in her bedroom, into a sort of crumpled curtsy like the princesses had done, waiting for the applause at having got the Munday family through yet another day.

But the rattling he could hear now was only the beginning of her day's performance; she had just come from the wings, as it were, with their eggs and bacon that he could smell. He heard the plates go down on the table and then the furious ring of the cowbell which the Munday family used as a gong. Breakfast was ready.

As Mark went hurriedly over to his basin the shiver of piano scales that he had been hearing unconsciously all the time stopped, but before he had even finished dabbing at himself with his damp face cloth and running his hands over the towel to dry them, it had begun again. That would be Evie, grabbing up her orange juice and apple, balancing them on the top of the piano as she went on. She was as thin as a bit of string anyway, but always trying to get thinner; particularly when she was in love. Not that she ever wasn't. There was always someone, either a real person or one out of a film or book – though she only bothered to get thin for the real ones – and at the moment it was her music teacher. Because of him she was now living in a perpetual shower of notes, like rain, trying to get so good at playing that he would notice and take her on a tour round the world with him, in a blissful sort of orbit for ever and ever more.

Evie's loves were a great trial to the rest of the family; it was like having someone perpetually sickening for measles, only with a longer quarantine. As Mark felt to see if there was still something which would pass muster as a handkerchief in his blazer pocket he heard Seb go in.

If only he had been given the same sort of clever beaky face as Seb! He took a last swift look in the mirror to see if his teeth would do. If only one of his eyebrows had been put higher than the other and one eyelid drooped a little lower, so that he had Seb's permanently witty sort of look! But it was no good, he thought enviously, as he went across the hall and into the dining-room, even if he had looked like his brother and his eyebrows gone up and down like anything nobody would ever have laughed at the dull things he said.

'Mark!' Tata caught hold of his collar and pulled him towards her, peering first into his face and then swiftly down his neck. 'Nottee! You wash after dressing, you no clean your teeths! After breakfast,' and she pushed him firmly down into his chair. Seb, delicately cutting at the crisp brown fringe of his egg, winked at him and from the next-door room came a furiously increasing crescendo of scales.

As Seb tapped his head and rolled his eyes up Mark giggled. Then, as Max Munday came in to breakfast, in his dressing-gown, he looked at his father shyly and grew quiet.

As always, his father smelt very clean and of a pleasant mixture of tobacco and lavender shaving soap; the faded brocade of his old dressing-gown sprawled richly with dragons. Although his slippers were well worn their red leather still looked fine and goodly, with a rich polish, as everything that he owned or wore always managed to do. As he heard the scales he too looked at Seb and shook his head in resignation.

Afraid, once again, that he wasn't going to be noticed; trying to gain time while he thought of something good to say, Mark buried his face in his cocoa mug: he often found food a convenient hiding place. But unluckily he had timed it wrong, for just as he had drawn in a large mouthful his father asked him a question.

'Hard at it already?' said Max Munday, with a slight look of disappointment when there was no answer forthcoming from his middle son, 'Well, never mind,' and by the time Mark had finished spluttering and could speak again his father had looked away and was talking to Seb.

So, as early as breakfast, there was the first blot on the day.

2

BREAKFAST over, Mark started on the journey downstairs, for school. It was a journey, too. The tall house had four floors and there were little landings between each, made, it always seemed to Mark, so that the stairs could stop and get their breath before they set out again, getting wider and better carpeted all the way down until they arrived in the splendid black and white marble squares of the hall.

If only they had one continuous lot of banisters so that he could have gone whizzing round and down; if only he could have turned them at will into a moving staircase! Plain stairs were so boring. At one time Mark used to pretend that they were steep rapids down which he could shoot his canoe but an attempt on a tray had unhappy results with the tenants.

Mr and Mrs Munday had rented this enormous house in Sicily Place when they first got married, which was before London had started sorting itself out again after the war. At that time a great bombed gap on one side of the house had made it look very unattractive and alarming cracks down the walls inside, with hanging flaps of wallpaper, had sent down the price. But now the cracks had been filled up again and a new house built next door and as the Mundays found themselves with a long, cheap lease in the expensive, doctors' part of London they considered themselves very lucky.

Different doctors rented the grand consulting rooms on the first two floors and by adding all the rents together the Munday family were able to go on living in the less splendid but more friendly and sunny rooms at the top. It suited Mr Munday, who liked plenty of space, and Mark's mother paid so little attention to her surroundings anyway that she always gave the impression that she was camping out. As they had two floors, there was plenty of room, Evie could play the piano in hers and Seb paint the walls of his own room black, luminous or whatever his craze was at the moment; play his oboe or rig up a projector for the cartoon films that he made.

Mark hopped down three steps on to the first half-landing, a quite difficult feat because they were at their steepest and narrowest here. When he was small he used to hate making the journey, up or down, because of the things that waited lurking on these landings. Like the Queen's Beasts, each flight had its different shaped monster, which would come thickening out of the dusk to do differently alarming things to him. But now he was older they seemed to have lost their power. After he had survived a few years of journeys and never actually been harmed he began slowly to wonder if they really could be so fierce after all and as his cockiness grew he took to shouting at them rudely as he went past. By the time he had been stopped doing this by the irate tenants he found that the monsters had shrivelled and shrunk away.

It was only on very rare occasions, such as Hallowe'en, or when it was foggy, that he still remembered them. Nowadays it was the actual humans, who lived about three to a landing, that he found more disturbing.

They were so dreadfully apt to pop out and say jolly and hearty things to passing children, expecting replies. This didn't worry Seb or Evie, who were never at a loss for an answer to shout back, nor the twins, who just stared, accepting all the attention they got with their bored, film-star expressions. But Mark always got caught. Unable to think of anything to say, he still felt it would be rude to go on until he had produced a remark and like a bird with its feet caught he would stand shifting from leg to leg until released. Far the worst of these waylaying chatterers was Dr Barth, on the first floor. Mark shivered as he crossed the next landing and started down towards it.

Perhaps it was because the others in the family went about in pairs that it was easier for them, thought Mark; perhaps if there had been two of him in the middle of the family, he would have been as easy and as back-chatting as anyone. Then both of them could have laughed together about Dr Barth and not been frightened. With his hand on the banisters now he went even more slowly down the widening stairs, reluctant to reach the dangerous territory.

Two of him; it was a good thought and he turned it round in his mind, like sucking a sweet. How he wished it were true! Would he like a brother, or sister, or what? Not another Munday, Mark decided quickly, whichever it was, or they'd be sure to come out clever again; not even a twin because Adam and Lucy had put him off those. Just a friend or a distant cousin perhaps, but in either case they'd have to be an orphan or have parents far abroad because he didn't want to share this other person; he wanted him entirely for himself.

As the banisters beneath his hand started flowering out

into the iron curlicues of the first floor his imagination started flowering out too and fitting possible faces on to this wish companion. Should it be a sort of double, someone like himself? No, for there wouldn't be any point if they weren't different, and unexpected. Someone like Riding or Hayhoe, at school? But, that wasn't any good either because if they had been going to be the ones he could have made friends with them already; they were quite good to scuffle around with but he didn't want either of them with him all the time. A girl? The face grew a pony tail and then quickly vanished; he wouldn't know what girls thought about and certainly didn't want one of them.

Tanned and springy-heeled, the explorer with the flashing blue eyes sprang temptingly before Mark's inner eye, jerking his head in an invitation to be followed, but that was no good either. Mark knew that it must be someone of his own age. Lost in the fascination of trying to make someone who was exactly right Mark stopped absent-mindedly where the stairs widened to their full splendour and became crimson-carpeted, and stood stock still.

It was rather like playing the game of 'Twenty Questions', he decided, as you threw away all the people who didn't fit, you got nearer to the one who did, but he hadn't got the answer yet. Animal, vegetable, mineral ... An animal would be jolly good. They didn't talk but just agreed with you and always thought you were quite splendid and absolutely right. As Mark stood thinking about the satisfactoriness of animals he didn't hear the door open down below.

Doubts grew again and he went on down a step or two. For did he really want to be agreed with all the time, even supposing that he had been allowed to keep a dog or anything at Sicily Place? He felt he wanted more than that, someone with the niceness of an animal but to share things with too, someone who would suggest things to do and sometimes argue with him in a friendly way. Someone who could tell him things and be interested in the things he told them, someone who, really, as well as everything else, would be like his father shrunk down a bit ...

'Well, young man! A penny for your thoughts!' The unpleasantly soft voice seemed to come suddenly from the wall directly opposite him and Mark nearly shot out of his skin.

Brought violently back into the present again he looked up in alarm. He saw that while he had been lost in thinking he had arrived on the very landing that he usually took such pains to hurry past, going on tiptoe and holding his breath. It had always been a bad one. In the old days the worst of the monsters, one called Pog Borius, had lived there, and now there was Dr Barth.

If Mark had just been trying to think up someone who had every quality that he did like then Dr Barth was just the other way round for he had everything that Mark hated. And the strange thing was that when the others teased Mark about his dislike he couldn't possibly explain why it was so strong. It just was.

There was Dr Barth's funny finger, of course, though Mark knew perfectly well that he couldn't help this and he didn't at all mind funny things in other people, such as Tata's knobbly legs and feet and the nice paper seller's purple nose. There was his voice and his eyes but it was really much more than either of these because it was the whole effect of him that was so unpleasant, too soft and too polite and pretending too hard to be interested in you all the time, when you knew that he couldn't possibly be. Mark always felt that he was like an actor, playing the part of somebody quite different, only actors made you believe in the other person and Dr Barth never did. It was like someone trying to hide behind a curtain when you could still see his horrible self bulging through.

'Ah, you're a very long way away! I see they must be

very deep thoughts!' The doctor's voice came out thickly like warm fudge from a pan, or a coil of garage grease. His eyes were oily too, and so dark that you couldn't see any pupils or expression in them as they peered out from his putty-coloured, thick-skinned face. It always seemed to Mark to have an indoors, grown-under-a-stone sort of look, as though the doctor lived only by central heating and electric light.

It really seemed that he did. On the one horrible time when Mark had got sucked into his room, like a tin tack into a Hoover, it had been most horribly hot and steamy, as though someone had just had a hot bath there without opening the window, and the windows themselves were so lost behind thick curtains that even at three o'clock in the afternoon all the lights had been on. The game which they were playing at Mark's school that term was thinking up what animals people were like, and he never saw Dr Barth without thinking of a great frog squatting on a lily pad in some murky, steamy pool.

Almost believing that he could see little wisps of steam come with him, Mark saw the doctor widen the crack and come right out through his doorway now, with his stocky, over-fat figure in its black suit outlined against it. He looked down at Mark. Holding tight on to the banisters behind him, getting again this hoovering feeling that he couldn't look away and was just about to be sucked in again, Mark gazed nervously back.

'What have you been thinking about, eh? Something important, I can tell.' As Mark stared back, trying to hold on to all his thoughts, like hats in a high wind, determined that Dr Barth should never get hold of a single one of them, the dreadful thing happened.

'I expect you are thinking about your father, aren't I right?' Like a bird pulling a worm out of the ground the doctor had managed to get Mark's last thought out! 'Well, I should too, if he were my father ... Mark wriggled at the

thought, '... He's soon going to be a very, very famous man. I expect you are thinking what a lucky boy you are!'

As those horrible eyes looked down at him, above the rubbery smile, Mark's nervousness suddenly turned to fury and he went cold all over. To have Dr Barth's stumpy fingers, especially that broken, dangling one, wandering about anywhere amongst his thoughts was bad enough, but to have him touching on the most special one ... to have someone like Dr Barth trying to guess at what he felt about his father!

'Oh, no,' he said, loudly and clearly, determined that at any cost Dr Barth should never know, 'I don't want to be like my *father*!' and the moment the words had floated off his lips all the doors of all the landings seemed to be opening everywhere. The front door swung open, the tenant doctors started to come in and go up the stairs to their rooms, and far up above him he heard the one special door of his father's study with its peculiar squeak open and then bang shut again. The whole house, even the whole street, Mark felt in his desperation, must have heard his denial. Feeling himself go scarlet to the roots of his hair he rushed down the remaining stairs and out of the still swinging front door. He had to run to the end of Sicily Place before he could feel that the rush of air had washed off the sticky feeling that Dr Barth always gave him.

But nothing could wash away the memory of the dreadful thing he had said. Had his father really been at the open door upstairs? Could he have heard? Oh, surely, things couldn't be as unfair as that! Even if his father hadn't been listening, would somebody else tell him what Mark had said? He'd bet that Dr Barth would; he would say it was his duty ... Just a busybody, that's what he was, thought Mark furiously, using children to worm his way into things that didn't concern him! In his rage a strong and curious feeling that he'd had once before came back to him. Although his father said that Dr Barth was a very clever man Mark didn't trust him, he never had. He didn't know what he was up to, but he was sure it wasn't good, nor did he even feel that Dr Barth really liked his father. He was too jolly flattering and smarmy about him all the time.

As Mark waited on the traffic island half-way across into the park he wriggled and squirmed so much to get rid of the thought of Dr Barth and his dangling finger, that an old woman looked down at him anxiously.

He grinned at her and felt slightly better. She was the sort of old woman he liked, the kind that seemed to have climbed up on to a nice peaceful island in life where everything was certain while everyone else was still swimming madly about in the sea. It was funny, too, how exchanging grins with someone, as though you had some secret understanding, made things seem not quite so bad. Oh, if only he had this friend of his to grin at! More than ever now Mark longed for someone and as his lights changed to green and he darted across to the other side of the road he started thinking about it all over again.

He would soon be at school, but how could you tell about what had happened to someone like Riding or Hayhoe? They would think he had gone clean, flittering, bats. How could he tell Jamie, even? Mark had reached the end of the Boat Lake now and thought of this exciting but much too glamorous friend. He sighed. Jamie was right out of Mark's world.

He wasn't there now, of course, because he would be on the way to his school too. But when Mark came home in the evenings Jamie, dressed in his tough blue jersey and thigh-length waders, would already be hard at work. His father owned and let out all the canoes and little boats on the lake and Jamie's job was to help him and the hired man push them off from the shore and whistle them back in again when their time was up. When boats got tangled up together in the middle it was his splendid job to wade out like Gulliver and disentangle them, and he knew all about engines and could quickly start the silent ones phut-phutting again.

When this hero had come over to Mark one day and started talking casually, leaning over the fence during a slack period, when he waved to him the next and then came over to talk all the following days Mark could hardly believe his luck. He dreamt of those waders and even developed a slightly nautical roll as though he himself were wearing them; he wished that he too could have a dark blue jersey that smelt of pond water, petrol and paint.

But although Jamie wasn't much older than Mark he was much more grown up and though they stayed friends it was a friendship which existed only in the park. Once outside it, Jamie went off back to a fascinating world of brightly lit streets and markets, of fish and chip shops, cafés with juke boxes and everyone shouting to each other up and down the houses and across the road. How warm and cosy it must be, thought Mark regretfully, considering the wide, well-behaved pavements of sedate Sicily Place.

'You live up there?' Jamie had said when Mark had pointed out their house to him, 'Cor!' and his expression was such that neither of them had ever mentioned it again.

Jamie's father and family full of uncles, Mark gathered, all owned boats which they hired out in the summer and side shows which they took round to the winter fairs; it seemed a splendid life to Mark because it was all to do with people enjoying themselves. Jamie certainly seemed to think it was the one and only life and pitied anybody else's. He was the one who did most of the talking, telling the wide-eyed Mark about all the rumbustious things that happened to him.

'And come the end of the summer I go hoppin',' Jamie had said the last time they met, as he caught hold of a boat by its painter and helped a fluttering small girl ashore, 'Down in Kent. Want a change from all this lot sometimes and you can make some good money there,' and, of course, as Mark listened about the hop gardens and the little cabins that the families camped out in, the sing-songs, the laughter and the good fellowship, it seemed as robust and jolly as every other aspect of Jamie's life.

How he wished he could join in that outside life of Jamie's. But he knew he never could. The friend he wanted would have to share everything and be with him all the time, not just in odd half hours. Still thinking of him Mark rounded the other end of the lake by the boathouse and went out through the far gate of the park. There was only one other road to cross now before he reached the school.

*

As Mark slid into his desk, just making it in time, he saw at once that something was up. The master's desk at the end of the room had been put very square and the blackboard beside it was very clean. The duster had been folded exactly into eight and some new, pointed bits of chalk put out on the ledge. He looked at Hayhoe beside him, squaring off all his books too, and fussily sharpening pencils until there was a row of little wooden ballet dancers' skirts in front of him. Mark raised his eyebrows in question and Hayhoe just had time to shuffle the sharpenings into the waste-paper basket, blow on his desk and whisper 'Governor's visit this afternoon – Old Jellybags, three o'clock!' before their form master came in.

There was to be a visit ('Stale buns!' muttered Hayhoe) that afternoon, from one of the school's most distinguished governors, Professor Jellicoe, he announced, and so that day's lessons would be altered a little. Instead of history in the classroom they would go on their Ancient History visit to the British Museum ('Wants to get us out of here and posh it up a bit!' hissed Riding from the other side) but Mark was hardly paying attention, for his eyes had lit up at the governor's name and the thought it had brought.

Professor Jellicoe was a friend of his father's and often came round to Sicily Place in the evenings to talk. If somehow Mark could manage to shine this afternoon, look super-tidy and super-bright and give the right answer to a question, he was pretty sure it would be reported back. Then, even if Dr Barth or someone else had repeated his awful, unmeant remark of this morning, it wouldn't seem quite so bad. Perhaps he could even get in somehow what he really thought about his father in some subtle sort of way (for he didn't mind Professor Jellicoe knowing), so that the professor would get the message across to Mr Munday and all Dr Barth's work might be undone. Hope sprang up again and Mark, full of it, started squaring off his desk too, squarer than any desk had ever been before.

3

WHEN the school bus got to the museum boys fell off it like beads from a broken necklace. Some scattered into the car park and some rolled up the steps outside the building and when Mr Bletchly got off the bus behind them there were even two or three boys sitting on the top parapet and one preparing to go in through the revolving entrance doors. Mr Bletchly was large, easy-going and beginning to run to fat and by the time he had got all their dark green forms collected tidily inside the hall he was thoroughly hot and exhausted. To recover himself he took them straight to the quiet, cool Assyrian room, and sank down on to a bench in the middle.

'*The Assyrian* ...' He looked in question at the throng of pink faces which were milling round him, making him feel even more dazed and sleepy than before.

'*... came down like the wolf on the fold,*' chanted the with-it ones. The rest, grateful for the lead, took up the chorus.

'*And his cohorts were gleaming in purple and gold* ...' they continued, though few of them had the slightest idea what cohorts were. Mark himself had a mistaken idea that they were the top part of someone's legs and imagined them clad in splendid armour.

As the chorus died down Mr Bletchly nodded, satisfied. He was popular, partly because his largeness slowed him up and made him good-natured and partly because he expected the best out of people and that they would know the right answer; he wasn't the sort that always tried to trip you up. He leaned back his head. The sun was coming pleasantly down through the glass above him and made him almost unbearably drowsy. With an effort he pulled himself upright again and looked at the boys.

'Good. Well, now that you remember about the Assyrians ...' A brilliant, comfortable idea had just come to him. '... I want you to spend some time looking at these carvings of them on the walls, which will show how they lived. I'll give you ...' He looked at his watch. Could he risk half an hour? No, they'd never stay harmless that long.

'... twenty minutes,' he said hopefully, 'then I shall ask you questions. I'll report the three most observant ones to Professor Jellicoe this afternoon. Off you go!' The idea of any sort of competition usually got them and kept them quiet for a while. With a peaceful sigh he leant back and shortly his large figure was as still as that of the attendant at the far end of the room, who seemed to be able to sleep standing.

The idea of a competition did get them and in the first few seconds everyone was determined to be as observant as a hawk and each one certain that he would win. They scurried away to the carvings and pushed one another aside as they glued their attention on the walls with great intent, noting down the long lines of funny-hatted little men toiling up mountains with baskets of stones, the guards on horseback watching them and the king in his chariot at the top. They noted the hunting scenes and the court scenes too and all might have gone well and Professor Jellicoe confronted with a whole form full of boys bursting with Assyrian information if Hayhoe, trying to go one better and get some extra gen, hadn't wandered off to one side to read what the description of a carving said.

'Tiglath ...' he began and then looked at the others in delighted astonishment, 'Tiglath Pileezer! That's the name of this king! Tiglath Pileezer – Ticklath the Teaser – Pickleth Pileezer!' and on this final outburst of long ee's he darted at a smaller boy and started tickling him under the arms till the victim collapsed on the floor, giggling and gasping for mercy. Hayhoe, joined now by Riding, started on somebody else. A slaughter like that done by the Assyrians now developed, till the floor was covered with giggling and faintly squeaking bodies rolling helplessly about over the gratings. But as the attendant had sleep-walked himself off to inspect a parallel gallery and the pleas for mercy were only squeaked out in agonised whispers Mr Bletchly still dozed peacefully on in the sunshine.

Mark, to whom tickling was death and who was too good-natured to inflict its agonies on anybody else, quickly followed the attendant and slipped round the corner.

Hayhoe and Riding must have skins like old boots, he thought, still clenching his arms tight against his sides so that their wriggling fingers wouldn't get in. Minds like old boots too, if they couldn't realise how much some people hated being tickled; he couldn't bear people who touched you when you didn't want to be touched. His friend wouldn't. His friend would know just how terrible and paralysing it was to have other people's great fingers prodding into you and have the tact not to do it. As the subdued noise of scuffling came nearer to the door Mark moved swiftly away down the long gallery he was in, his thoughts drawn back towards this super-friend again.

This gallery was full of enormous statues, so that it was like being in a stone wood. As Mark wandered alone between them he found himself first beside an enormous pair of human legs, with each toenail the size of his hand, and then by gigantic bull's legs with hooves that he could have sat on. But as he followed their carved surfaces upwards he saw to his surprise that they had somehow got mixed, there was a bull's head on top of the man's legs and a solemn man's face, bearded and crowned, coming up from the bull's shoulders. As he looked round, he saw that this seemed to be happening all over the place.

It was like an immense game of heads, legs and bodies and Mark was fascinated. Forgetting Tiglath and the teasers he wandered on happily down the long room, looking first at one statue and then at another. After he had been doing this for a while, drifting along between the long shafts of sunlight, a strange feeling began to come over him.

Usually statues in a museum were just statues and it was jolly hard to imagine anyone making them or putting them up in the desert, or wherever it was. But as Mark looked up at these, and perhaps it was because he was still half-thinking of his friend, he slowly began to understand what their makers must have had in their minds. As he stared at a feathery leg it suddenly came clear to him. Those old carvers had been doing just the same as he had and trying to think up friends of their own too, giving them all the bits of anything, man or bird or animal, that they liked best! It was such an astonishing thought that he sat down plop on a bench and stared open-eyed at an old professor who had already parked himself there, contemplating a winged ibex. The old man winked at him, then got up and walked away.

After a minute or two Mark himself got up again and moved on among the forest of strange creatures. He was more critical now. Most of them weren't at all what he himself would have chosen, but he could see what the carvers were aiming at. As well as the statues with men's heads and great powerful bull's bodies, with wings for good measure, there were plain winged lions and winged ordinary men. A lot of wings, and about this part Mark agreed. They would certainly be a good thing if you were allowed to choose anything you liked. But some of the carvers must have had funny ideas as well. There was one man with a baboon's head and another whose body was topped by a ram's head with great curling horns; there were bird-headed men that Mark didn't care for at all. Apart from the fact that he couldn't see the point of just having the head of a bird, if you couldn't fly

as well, the beaks made them look cruel and rather mean.

There was a hippopotamus goddess, carved out of some sort of stone which looked like corned beef and a little figure with a frog's face that he moved away from quickly because it reminded him of Dr Barth. There were quite a lot of plain men among the mixtures and plain animals too, particularly lions. There were all sorts of these, proud lions, and sleepy ones, good-tempered lions and long-suffering ones like those in Trafalgar Square. There were cross lions as well, and peevish hawks and bad-tempered rams and gazelles. Funny to have a peevish friend! But as he was thinking this suddenly, right at the end of the gallery, Mark found the best creature of all, someone who had a lion's head and a lion's tail swishing down beneath a sort of tunic affair, a man's body, but with feathers down its neck, and horse's ears; a man's legs with great iron muscles in them and lion's claws at the end. This seemed like having the best of all worlds and Mark was just moving round behind it to see if it had folded-up wings as well when he heard the whistle that was Mr Bletchly's rallying call.

Oh, gosh, and he was supposed to be there, knowing all about the King of Assyria's little basket-carrying men! He had wanted to do so well and he had completely forgotten. But perhaps he would manage somehow. Cross with himself but full of hope Mark dashed back down the gallery, dodging the sightseers and the woken-up attendant and feeling vaguely that winged gods, bulls and lions, with even his own friend somewhere among them, were all flying, flapping and padding along beside him. A few of them still seemed to be round him as he skidded in to join the rest of the party, too breathless to speak.

Mr Bletchly, completely unaware that he had done anything more than close his eyes to rest them, or that a devastating carnage had been going on round his senseless form, was only rather surprised that twenty minutes of observing Assyrians could have such an odd effect on collars, ties and hair. But he passed it by and was pleased when he started asking his questions and a forest of smug hands went up in reply.

'... What animals were in the hunt? ... what weapons did the warriors have? ... What were the men pulling on ropes for? That's right – to lever a statue up. What sort of a pulley were they using ... do we ever see anything like that nowadays? ...'

'Please sir! Please sir! Please sir!' The hands of Roseburn, Hart and Watkins shot up and down like pistons as Mr

Bletchly mentally chalked up marks to them. The others sighed. It was no good counting those three; they always won.

Then there was a question about the old winged-bull statue that the little men had been hauling up. Desperate for glory and feeling that he knew this bull as well as one of his own family by now Mark shot up his arm but he was too breathless to be able to get the words out before half a dozen other boys shouted him down. Oh, bother! In his disappointment he half turned, as though to his imaginary friend, for consolation; he had so much wanted to be mentioned to Professor Jellicoe!

But as he let his arm down again in disappointment he suddenly jumped like a jack-in-the-box and snatched it up again swiftly, catching Hayhoe a smart clout on the chin as he did so.

'Mark Munday! What are you doing? You're not paying attention again!' but the words broke over Mark unheeded, as did Hayhoe's retaliating attempts to start tickling him. For Mark was looking down at his fingers, and then at the floor.

There was nothing there, of course there couldn't be, he thought slowly; dogs weren't allowed in the Museum. But the first time he had put his hand down, thinking of his friend, he could have sworn that it had fallen into thick, warm, living fur.

4

THE surprise in Mark's mind and this strange sensation in his fingertips lasted all the way back to school; it was a tingling, electric sort of feeling and he wondered if there was going to be a storm. It was funny, he thought, going to a museum must be rather like going to a cinema. It always took a little while before you stopped being Ben Hur, or the Sheriff, or whoever it was, and now, in the intervals of ragging with the others, he still seemed to be vaguely aware of furry and feathery things all round him, of little men humping bricks about and these statues from old Tiglath's day.

But as they trooped up to the top deck of the bus and Mark just beat Riding to the front seat, he forgot museum, dogs and everything else as he plonked himself down and went through the motions of driving the bus at enormous speed and with superlative skill, giving himself special powers to go the wrong way up one-way streets and the backwards way round roundabouts. The only shreds left of his morning's museum-viewing were when he felt the bus grow enormous wings to lift itself out of some sudden difficulty and trail feathered feet that happily snatched off hats and helmets, flinging them away to bowl through the streets like autumn leaves. When they got off and started back along the pavements to school Mark found it difficult to bring himself down into an ordinary, walking human again.

It was lucky for the school that old Jellybags wasn't coming to inspect lunch, he thought, a little later, because it was a dreary affair of fish cakes, prunes and custard. When the last yellow and purple-streaked blob had been swilled down by the last mouthful of water the boys' bottled-up energy burst out. There was an infantile craze that week for spinning knives round and asking them questions and soon the table was a whirling clatter of blades.

'Who's the ugliest chap ... whose ears stick out most ... who's going to flunk the exams ... It's Gandy ... no, it isn't ... oh, you cheated! You thumped the table and made it move an inch more! Well, you are the most clotted one, anyway ...'

In the middle of it all Mark got bored and started playing with his knife on his own. If you held it on your forefinger, he discovered, with the blade and the handle balanced, like the middle walls of a card house, it would stay hovering there. He tried a dive-bombing zoom with it, but the blade-wing dipped into his plate, and the whole thing clattered down, spattering prune juice. He tried again.

In the meantime, having used up all the insulting questions he could think of, irritating Hayhoe had started off again with a fresh series of twiddlings, this time to ask rude questions about people's families. It was just about as stupid an idea as his tickling had been, thought Mark disgustedly; it was like tickling people's minds. The trouble about Hayhoe was that he never knew when to stop. As Mark thought of his prodding and wriggling fingers he suddenly remembered Dr Barth and his horrible one. Looking round for fresh fields to disturb, Hayhoe knocked the delicately balancing knife off Mark's finger and spun it round to cry:

'Whose father's got the funniest job?'

'I don't know whose father has,' said Mark scornfully, 'but I know who will have when they're grown up. You will! You'll be a psychi ... a psycho ...' He couldn't have spelt it in a month of Sundays but that was what Dr Barth said he was.

'A what? Cor, listen to Munday! Listen to the words he knows!' and before Mark could say anything more Hayhoe had turned the tables on him and the rest of the herd had gone with him too. Somehow it always seemed to happen this way; by tomorrow the rest of the form would forget again and be quite friendly but for the moment they were after him like dogs after a hare.

The knife spun and then stopped, spun and stopped as the blade was flicked towards Mark and the hurting questions came bursting out.

'Who's got the brother who's most like a parrot ... a sister who's soft on the bandmaster ... whose mother wears the soppiest hats ...' They were imitating Seb's funny voice, his mother's accent, Evie's ...

'Shut up, Hayhoe!' Mark got to his feet, scarlet. It was true that his mother had come to the last Speech Day in a lemon yellow hat like an upside-down basket, it was true that Evie had hung love-lorn round the bandstand all last summer, but it wasn't their business and they weren't going to laugh!

'Munday! It's Munday! Who's father got ...'

'Shut up!' He didn't know what they were going to say, but they weren't to say it! They weren't even to mention his father! Mark was suddenly quite alone, fighting to defend his family against the whole silly lot of them. He lost his temper and crashed both hands down on the table so that the spinning knives jerked up in the air and then fell clattering down into the plates, sending custard, prune stones and odd bits of food all over the place.

Mark was so furious that he hadn't noticed Mr Bletchly come up behind him and the other boys tactfully step back from the table, leaving him with both hands flat on a criss cross of messy knives and with a red face spattered with yellow and purple flecks.

'Munday! You again! What's come over you today? Now really, this is too bad of you!' Agitated out of his usual mildness by the thought of the governor's visit even old Bletchly was bleating away, his bow tie wobbling. 'When we particularly want everything to be clean and shipshape! Now go and get something to wipe those marks off the tablecloth,' and Mark, who had reckoned on the free time after lunch to mug up his English for the Professor's inspection, went furiously off to get a cloth.

It was no good, he thought despondently, as he scrubbed away at the custard and prune marks, he couldn't win either way. At home his family thought him too dull and ordinary and at school, because of his family, they thought him too unordinary. He didn't belong anywhere. Back into the ditch of self-pity again he remembered that dreadful story about how it you let a tame bird out of a cage wild birds would come and attack it (though his father said it wasn't true) and as he rubbed at one particularly difficult prune-juice spot, he saw himself dramatically as some ill-fated canary or budgerigar.

But, in the odd way things do, the very thought cheered him up. All right then, so he was a canary. The rest were only stupid sparrows, anyway, and he would far rather be something different, on his own. And wouldn't he jolly well show them this afternoon what sort of a family he did come from, wouldn't he outshine them all! English was his best subject, whether he'd had time to mug it up or not – he'd show them! And Professor Jellicoe would go home and tell his father how bright he had been and so Mark would be able to show them at home too. Everything seemed fine again.

Well, that was as clean as he could get it. Putting a salt cellar over the worst spot, now a depressing sort of pale mauve and the shape of Ireland, Mark pushed his chair back from the table. And then he suddenly shot to his feet, for something had seemed to swish and curl round his legs. What *was* going on today? Remembering what had happened in the museum, Mark put out a hand and looked down. For a moment he seemed to feel a quick, faint tingle in his fingertips but once again there was nothing there, only the fold of the large tablecloth swishing into place.

How funny! But after a minute or two Mark's thoughts went back to the comfortable place where they had been basking. That's right; he'd show them: he'd show everybody. The idea was so pleasant that as the bell rang and he rushed off from the cleaned cloth towards the classroom he quite forgot to take the yellow splashes off his own face

'Well boys! Good afternoon.' Professor Jellicoe acknowledged the form's prim greeting and motioned them to sit down. As his eyes wandered along their faces he recognised Mark's but looked again in surprise before he gave him a brief little extra nod.

So that was all right; the Professor had noticed him. Oblivious of the custard, Mark smoothed down his hair and tried to keep all his attention together so that he would shine as he had planned. He remembered that his father had once tried to teach him an exercise about this and he was determined to put it into practice. Think of your mind as a greyhound, Mr Munday had said, a greyhound behind a wire starting gate, and then let it out after one idea, and one idea only, like a hare, so that it chases after it down one alley. But on the few previous occasions that Mark had tried he had been depressed to find that his mind seemed more like a cage full of grasshoppers. Instead of one big idea he seemed to have dozens of tiny ones which jumped about in all directions and squeezed themselves through the wires ... or just sat chirping inside ... oh, dear, he was at it again. Manfully he tried to focus on the greyhound and to hold it on a leash.

'I'm going to give you questions from your anthology,' Mr Bletchly was holding up the familiar volume of poetry and they all shuffled dutifully among their books and brought that one up to the top, beaming over its edge.

'Now ...' Mr Bletchly looked down at the register and Mark held on to his greyhound, 'Ancaster. What do you know of the battle of Chevy Chase?'

The lucky squirt! Anyone could remember what happened in that one! Ancaster's rendering was unnecessarily helped on by a whispered chorus, rising like kettle steam from all round him.

'Good boy.' Mr Bletchly looked down the register again and picked on names here and there, giving them one easy poem after another. Partly out of decency and partly for the honour of the form he was being as kind as he could; if the poems weren't easy ones he always managed to help with some little clue, like the people who give away the prizes on the TV. For the first few minutes Mark managed to keep on the alert then, as Mr Bletchly's pencil hovered first over the beginning of the alphabet and then the end Mark, feeling safely in the middle, as though he were in the dry part under the Niagara Falls, felt his attention starting to wander. Instantly as though the greyhound in his mind had felt the leash slacken a little, it started shuffling round with its long nose in odd corners.

First of all Mark thought about Professor Jellicoe's face and what funny purple-red vein marks it had on it, rather like the prune stains, then he remembered him coming out of his father's study at home; he heard their two voices together and seemed to smell his father's special tobacco, leather and shaving soap smell. From that he wandered on to the squeakiness of blackboards and of the fineness of the afternoon outside the window, of Jamie and his boats and of the queer drive back from the museum that morning.

'... "*Earth has not anything to show more fair* ..." Eversley. Who said that and where was he standing when he said it?'

'On ... Was he standing on a peak, sir? Yes, a peak in Darien!'

The rest of the form clucked and tittered righteously and Eversley fell. The droning of names went on, some doing well and some badly.

Mark's errant mind had strayed far away by now; it had gone back right into the museum and was remembering the furry, feathery feeling he'd had when he came out, as though some of those strange creatures had come prowling out after him.

'Plumstead.

> "... *He clasps the crag with crooked hands*
> *Close to the sun in lonely lands* ..."'

Mark nodded to himself. Yes, there had been eagles there

too. They wouldn't have been his choice for friends, they were too fierce and beaky, but everyone to his taste, and he still had this odd feeling that, just as it had been for those old carvers, somewhere there might be something that exactly suited him. In his comfortably dreamy state he could almost begin to see and feel it; strong but not too big ... just coming to his fingertips, like a large dog, would be a comfortable size he thought ... soft, padding, swishy ... with a waving tail that might disarrange table-cloths ... splendid whiskers ... but with human thoughts. The idea was taking hold of him so fast that he could almost see the creature in front of him, looking at him with eyes that glowed with affection and sparkled like a cat's eyes in the headlights of a car ... green ...

'"*Tiger, tiger, burning bright* ..." Munday. What animal is contrasted ... Munday! Did you hear me? I'll repeat the question ...'

'*Tiger, tiger* ...' But of course! The whole glorious beast sprang into life and with it Mark sprang to his feet.

'Yes, sir, of course, sir: that's him!' he almost shouted, beaming at everyone, and felt so pleased with himself that it was quite a minute before he took in Mr Bletchly's worried face and the professor's puzzled one and the fact that there was nothing there in front of him after all; before he realised that he ought to have been saying something about a lamb, a fact over which the rest of the sniggering form quickly put him to rights.

'Oh, sir, ...'

'Yes, yes; all right, Munday; you'd better sit down again.'

It was like the light going out and the glory of the great tiger went out with it, fading into a daydream that Mark could hardly remember, as all the old worries flowed back in. Because now his last chance of shining in front of Professor Jellicoe and having it reported to his father was gone; gone too was the last chance of getting anything but a major blowing up from anybody.

5

IT was quite impossible to tell Jamie. As Mark leant over the sun-baked rails and watched the sun glittering on the water he tried several times and then gave up. He wouldn't understand. Everything in Jamie's world just *was*, and nobody ever had to bother about thinking why or wondering if they were clever, or too ordinary. They expected everyone to be themselves and left it at that. Jamie worked for his father as a matter of course and his father never thought that Jamie would do anything else. It was as easy as that and it must be very peaceful.

Mark looked at Jamie, leaning beside him. He was large and tough and had a nice brown, wooden look, as though he had been carved out of some solid and lasting material. Mark shifted his own elbows on the rail and sighed.

Still, in spite of all his troubles, it was decent out here in the sun, smelling the water and not thinking of anything in particular, and he stared at the wash made by a motor-boat, at the gold-barred, rippling stripes.

Rippling stripes – tiger ... No, he didn't want to think about that. He didn't know what had come over him. If only he could have kept hold of his mind as he had meant to; if only he could have obeyed his father's greyhound rules! But now ... The best he could hope for was that the professor wouldn't say anything at all about him, either good or bad; the worst ... The other boys hadn't failed to point out to him how very peculiar his face had looked, all covered in custard blobs and bits of prune, and after what he had said ... And all of that to be added to what Dr Barth might have said about this morning. Oh, dear, he was getting in deeper and deeper, his father would never think he was anything but hopeless, ever again! Mark gave another great sigh and Jamie turned round.

It might not be possible to talk to Jamie but he had a rough and silent instinct for knowing when things weren't right; to him people were like boat engines and when they began to go wrong he could somehow sense it. His family didn't go in for words, they did things; if one of them had a bit of bad luck the rest would rally round in the ways they thought would be most helpful but nothing would be said. In the late afternoon the lake was fairly empty and the best little vessel, a beautiful rowing-boat, lay empty and rocking lightly in the wash of each successive boat that came home from its last trip. She was painted white and blue and the oars were blue with red bands round them; she was handy and trim and the apple of Jamie's eye. He had never been known to let a girl go out in her and only boys of whom he thoroughly approved; now he motioned Mark towards her with his head.

'Go on,' he said, 'you take her out. Needn't pay, we'll stand you for once. Go to the island, why don't you?' and he bent to hold her steady while Mark got in.

It wasn't any good trying to express his gratitude, nor would Jamie have liked it. Mark just looked at him, and then, 'Couldn't you come too?' he asked.

Jamie shook his head. 'There's still a few to come in – might join you later,' and he pushed Mark out into the shimmering lake.

Mark pulled away lustily, multiplying the arrow-headed ripples to either side of him and sending the ducks skimming off so that they added small new V-shaped patterns of their own. As he lay on the oars for a moment, after the first burst of energy, he watched one of the patterns grow wider and wider and wondered if it would eventually meet itself again, or go on forever. Infinity. As he thought of that bewildering thing he was back in the classroom and among all his troubles again. He wondered where things had started to go wrong and decided once again that it was this business of not having a greyhound mind.

He couldn't keep it along one track, it wasn't any use trying. Even now he was thinking partly of Mr Bletchly talking about infinity and making that funny little squiggle on the board, partly of Hayhoe sniggering, partly of Jamie being so decent and partly of how to catch hold of a willow branch on the ever-nearing island, so that he could land. But as he pulled himself in among the grey-green leaves he stopped thinking altogether in the practical problems of the moment.

He tied the little boat to a branch and then hauled himself up by a slim, slippery trunk until he was standing on the island, above the tiny inlet, all alone. Robinson Crusoe, Blackbeard the Pirate, the Swiss Family Robinson; he was each and all of them in turn. Living here in a goatskin tent, feeding off the land; monarch of all he surveyed. Delighted, he looked round.

There were so many thick-growing, long-pointed leaves all round him that it was like being in a thicket of green feathers. He couldn't even see the sky above him and the air was full of a sappy, willowy, pale-green sort of smell. He moved on a little, so that he was standing in the exact middle of his kingdom. When one of the little evening breezes came ruffling down the river it lifted and fluttered all the leaves for a moment, then they settled down again with a small muttering sigh.

Mark sat down on a low branch and sighed too, for as the breeze had turned up all the undersides of the leaves so it had flicked all the bothering thoughts back into his mind again. It was no good: even here, on this desert island, his worries still kept licking round him like the breeze; he just had to get things sorted out and decide what to do. It was all very well to moon about out here, putting off the time of going home, but soon he would have to go back, right into the heart of the trouble.

They wouldn't worry about him being late, that was one of the advantages of not having a tea-time mother, but the bad time would be when he did go in, past the open door of his father's study. With Dr Barth probably coming out, he thought, licking his lips in the horrible way he did, like a cat who had just been at the cream. Dr Barth and his father often discussed things together and Mark felt sure that he would have slipped in his little piece about Mark's rudeness and ingratitude. Then his father would come out too, look at Mark in a worried way and call him in, or, which would be even worse, look at him and say nothing at all. Mark hated it when his father's face got that expression.

If only things had gone as he meant! If only he could have been the first to rush in with good news, telling his father how he had won the museum competition and known all the English he was asked; if only for once he could have made his father feel pleased with him! He tried to picture this seemingly impossible situation and thought dolefully how dreadful it must be for his father, so special and clever, to have such a stupid, ordinary, perpetually disappointing son as himself. But he *had* known that poem, inside out, he really had!

'*Tiger, tiger* ...' The willow leaves quivered again and Mark felt a shiver go down his own back too. How could he have been so stupid when he knew it so well! It was just that he'd been thinking about this friend, wanting someone to talk all the puzzling things over with; someone whose eyes would look at you sympathetically, understandingly ... 'burning bright'.

The leaves started to lift again as though they had heard the stronger gust of wind that was coming down the lake; grey turned to silver and silver to little moving flames of white. As Mark started to say the poem over to himself he remembered the sudden strange and glorious feeling it had given him, like recognising something, that feeling which had made him gape and stare like a lunatic and driven every single other thought out of his head.

'*... in the forests of the night ...*' The wind had arrived full force now and the leaves all round were really agitated, moving in the whirlpool of a hundred criss-cross directions; flapping, fluttering, tiptoeing like a host of furred and feathered things from the museum, whispering and laughing as his friend would laugh and whisper, that friend he needed – oh so badly! – now.

Mark's want was so strong that it all went into a sort of knot in the middle of his forehead. He stood up and as he did so the leaves lifted their narrow hands all round him, breaking the dense curtain to let through the rosy evening light, so that it flickered in stripes of gold and orange and lay along their shivering white undersides, lighting the black bars of their twigs. So that it shone gooseberry green through a great solemn pair of eyes which were looking at Mark; looking at him, into him, through him ...

6

AS Mark stared back, quite empty with astonishment, he saw an animal grow round the eyes. And then in front of him, there on that ordinary island, came something so wonderful and magnificent that just to look at it made all his insides turn to smoke and his legs feel weak as water.

It was like the tiger in the poem and yet far, far better; it was like all those great beasts in the museum rolled into one. For a fleeting moment Mark seemed to see something of lion and something of splendid human in it too. But it was mainly tiger, he thought, when he could begin to do any sort of thinking again, mainly the most glorious superb tiger that anyone had ever thought of. And then, as he gazed on into the glowing green eyes, it began to change again.

Well, it wasn't a change exactly, but a sort of settling; from towering above him like the greatest of all the stone animals the beautiful creature was bringing itself down into a comfortable, friendly size. Almost, Mark thought unbelievingly, as though it wanted to fit itself to him; almost, though he hardly dared believe it, as though this glorious thing had come there specially for him.

'But of course I have!'

One of the green eyes winked.

'You called, didn't you?'

With the deepest surprise Mark realised that it was actually talking to him, though it didn't use anything that you could call a voice. It was just that he could feel the words coming into his mind, as warm and pleasant as hot water running into a bath. It was an absolutely wonderful feeling, the way everybody ought to talk to each other always, and although Mark couldn't hear any sound with his outside ears he knew what the voice was like, a rich sort of rumble like the notes of an organ when they shake the floor.

The animal seemed to be suggesting that Mark should sit down, but there wasn't any need for Mark was still so limp with the wonder and surprise that he collapsed down on to the branch again as though he was a folding chair.

In one easy movement the tiger sank down too, and from the great, curled-round paws at which Mark was now looking, padded and furry and flexing their well-sheathed claws in and out like those of some immense cat, he looked up again at the whiskered face.

'That's right. Get to know me: friends should.' Did one of those blazing green eyes lower a lid again and wink at Mark? As the tiger settled down comfortably he shot out a bright pink tongue and started licking at a small piece of twig which was caught up in the fur round one foot. Mark loosened the grip of his fingers on the bark beneath him. Gulping nervously, but feeling a wild sort of joy growing inside him, he did now dare to take a full and searching look.

The long body lay relaxed under the willow leaves and as they sent quivering shadows across it, the black-edged stripes seemed to flicker too; orange and tawny, sandy and white. The white fur shone softly as though it had just been washed and so did the long pale-gold guard hairs which sprang out from the black and marmalade stripes. The animal's whole coat was so shining with health and so loosely rippling that Mark felt he could have taken it up in handfuls if he tried. If he dared! He looked shyly at the face.

Black stripes barred the orange forehead too, like the wrinkles of someone who laughs a lot, and the ears curving outwards from his forehead were sharp and pointed. Where their tips curled under Mark saw that they were lined with thick white stuff, like the inside of a bean pod. He longed to put a finger in to feel and as though the animal had read his thoughts it flickered one ear down with a little noise like a flapping sheet and looked up from licking a paw.

Outlined first in black and then in white, like one of Evie's film stars, and with rising flames of eyebrows above them, the shining eyes looked back at Mark. They were green as glass, as mysterious as the deep part of a river, yet still with the suggestion of a smile and a wink, and there was this something else quite astonishing in them too. It was an expression of recognising and belonging, of being something that was only for Mark. With the utmost difficulty, because he felt that he wanted to go on gazing into those eyes for ever, he looked away to finish his examination.

A long nose sloped down to quivering pink nostrils; beneath them was the open mouth, still panting as though the tiger had come quickly from a long distance away. To either side of the furry chin sprang out magnificent whiskers that were wider than the whole face itself and there was a ruff of

white fur, each hair shining, outlining its edge. Ivory teeth, a curling vermilion tongue ... but Mark couldn't keep his eyes away from the animal's any longer; fascinated, he looked back again and saw the black upright slits in the green stretch wider and rounder.

'You'll know me next time!' The deep voice was lazy and amused as it came rumbling out, and once again, although Mark could hear it quite well, he couldn't tell whether it was a real voice at all or something he was imagining.

'N ... next time?' He had found his own voice at last but it came out in a whisper. Could this wonderful thing really happen again?

The tiger nodded.

'Why not? When you want. If you really want, that is. I come when you call.' He turned his head sideways to snap at a fly.

'I ... ?' Mark still could only stammer. *He* had called up all this splendour, this majestic creature? 'I did?' he asked again, like an idiot.

The tiger caught his fly, then nodded.

'But where do you come from? How do I call?' It was like this old business of being told you did something like fidgeting or looking sulky when you hadn't the faintest idea you were doing it. Except that this was the other way round because it was the good thing that you did without knowing.

'You call me by wanting ...' the tiger repeated; he obviously didn't care about having to make explanations and was growing bored, 'A special, strong kind of wanting ... I think ... I don't know ... there seem to be rules about it. I've been very near to you once or twice but then I have to go again; it's no good unless you can get right through.' He got up and stretched himself, then he looked back at Mark.

'But where are you all the time?' asked Mark again,

slightly more at his ease, 'Where do you wait in between times, till I call?' It was all so strange and baffling.

The tiger grew vague. 'Ah,' he began and looked puzzled, as someone well might who had only just been summoned from whatever splendid desert he lived in and found himself talking to a boy on a willow island. 'But the main thing is that you've done it. Don't let's waste time in case it gets undone again!' and he rose and padded a step or two towards Mark.

If the tiger had looked superb when he was sitting, the sight of him standing was beyond description. His burnished coat shone in shimmers of gold as the muscles moved beneath it. His straight, strong legs brought him up to the level of Mark's hips, just the size Mark had wanted, and his tail curled out behind him like a lasso thrown out in the air. Looking at Mark with amused affection, but in a most glorious, equal way, as one friend to another, he bent his head down so that Mark could see the springy hairs on the forehead and feel the wiry whiskers against his leg.

It was all so astonishing that Mark giggled a little as the whiskers tickled him and then suddenly he lost all his nervousness and did the thing that he had been longing to do all the time. He stuck his finger down one of those furry ear linings and in mock anger the golden beast turned and pretended to snap at him, as though his finger were a fly.

Delighted, Mark tried for the other ear and was just feeling the first touch of its furriness when a square paw came up and softly cuffed him aside. He rolled over on the twiggy ground and then there was fur rolling beside him, warm, fresh-smelling fur. For some minutes they wrestled and struggled and fought each other and it was like football and running full pelt and swimming and diving and all the other good, active things Mark had ever done all rolled into one. At last they came the right way up again, both panting and laughing and leaning against the fallen willow tree stump.

Mark gave a last thump at the white chest, and saw that he had turned one of the tiger's ears inside out. It shook its head to put it right.

But it . . . he . . . He couldn't go on calling such a personal tiger 'it', a friend who was so much more than just a tiger anyway.

Completely at his ease now, feeling that everything in the world was most absolutely and perfectly right, Mark leant against a branch beside his companion.

'You must have a name,' he said in this comfortable sort of think-talk, 'What is it?'

'A name? Well of course I have; I . . .'

'Mark! Hi, Mark!' There was a sudden shout from the water's edge. The tiger sprang lightly to his feet and froze, his long tail tense.

'It's Jamie! I'll have to go. Tell me quickly, what are you called and when shall I see you again?' Mark clutched at a handful of fur to make sure that his friend was still there and still real, for somehow he knew that it was part of these mysterious rules that the animal must go now.

'It's all right, I'm coming!' Mark shouted back.

'M . . .' The rumble of the voice, the feel of the fur were fading, the stripes flickering back in amongst the willow leaves again.

'An M like his! Mid . . .' What was it that Mark heard and where was he hearing it from? 'Mid w a y . . .' and there was suddenly nothing but a long shiver through the willow leaves. Mark ran to the bank above the inlet and looked down at Jamie, in another boat, rocking very gently on the calm lake.

There was a violent shudder through the leaves beside him, as though something large had sprung out of them and for a moment Mark thought that the waters beside Jamie's boat had parted and spread into rings, but the boat stayed quite still.

'What you lookin' at?' said Jamie, 'Swan takin' off; fish risin' or summat? I never saw nothing!' He looked up in mystification and now as Mark looked at the waters beyond Jamie's head they seemed to close up again in one enormous gooseberry-green wink. He laughed out loud.

'Whatever's come over you?' asked Jamie, 'I thought you was feelin' down!' But he was pleased to see Mark in such good spirits, the loan of his boat seemed to have done the trick. 'What you got in your hand, then? You can't row and hold on to something, you know...'

As Mark climbed down into the boat again he loosened his clutching fist. Did something white and shining flash across the water as Jamie unshipped the oars again? Mark thought he saw it blow away.

'Dandelion puff,' he said evasively, but Jamie only looked at him curiously.

'I didn't see anything,' he said.

7

IT was lucky there wasn't much traffic on the short way home because Mark felt as dazed as though he had been looking straight at the sun, much too dazzled to think properly.

Midway! Could there really have been a tiger and had it really said that? It seemed impossible, but though the animal had gone now he had somehow managed to leave the feeling of himself behind. Warm and glorious it was there beside Mark on the traffic islands, padding with him across the roads. As the companion he had longed for would, as his own friend – and what a friend! Happiness swelling and swelling inside him as he thought of it, so that he couldn't walk ordinarily but had to strut and sway and throw his arms about, Mark seemed to sense a striped form slipping in and out between the lines of cars, sleeker and stronger than they were and holding them back with the flick of a tail and a contemptuous paw.

A policeman's hand, clapped hard down on his shoulder, brought him back into the world of boring reality again.

'You gone colour blind all of a sudden? Can't you see those lights are red?' but Mark had only been seeing those brilliant green eyes, brighter than any traffic light that ever was. Green eyes and rippling stripes ... he blinked and stood guiltily beside the policeman till the lights turned and he was safe on his own home pavement side again.

But when would he see his friend really and actually again; how could he bring him back? 'Midway! Midway!' Mark called softly, but nothing appeared. No swishing tail, no fur at his fingertips, nothing at all. What had he done to get him? How could he call him again?

Going along the pavement he tried to remember back to the island. What was it that Midway had said? Ordinary life was coming back so strong now that it was all getting mixed up in his mind. Oh, what was it that he had been doing and thinking at the moment Midway appeared? How had he, dull, stupid Mark, managed to call up anything so wonderful?

The thought was so astonishing that Mark found he had arrived back at Sicily Place without noticing how he got there at all.

At the sight of the familiar door the troubles that had gone clean out of his head since the island came back. As though his words had somehow got frozen and were hanging about in the air like icicles, waiting for him, Mark could hear again the dreadful thing he'd said about his father just before he rushed out that morning. Had his father heard? Or if he hadn't, would Dr Barth have told him? There didn't seem much hope to Mark that he could have escaped both.

As all these bothers flew into his head and started buzzing round there like bees in a bottle, there was a sort of click in Mark's mind and a horrible dropping feeling, as though he had lost or forgotten something. He shook his head and looked up again.

Putting off the moment of going in Mark looked at the green paint and the shape of the sun blisters, then at the flaking gold of the number painted up above the door. After that, as he still didn't seem to have gathered enough courage he made himself look at the newly polished brass name-plates. This was another thing, like that impossible greyhound, which his father always told them to do. If you were nervous, he said, the best thing to do was to choose something quite ordinary and look at it very carefully, count all the scratches, notice the shape of the holes, the size of the dents; compare them with each other. If you did that, he promised, your mind would get focused on those and you'd quickly forget your own troubles.

It really did work and whenever he remembered to do it Mark would sit examining something like the different shaped whorls on his two thumbs while the rows and pep talks of irritated teachers thundered on overhead, though this wasn't quite the way in which his father had meant him to apply his advice. And as Mark looked at the shining strips of brass now his troubles certainly did seem to fade into the background. He kept concentrating on the brass plates and as he did so he thought that it was funny how things got like their owners. Some of the plates were pleasantly old and smooth and as kind as the doctors they belonged to, while others, particularly that of Dr Barth, were too bright and brashly and aggressively new.

'Well, here goes, then,' Mark said to himself, 'Better get it over,' and because he didn't take the key with him when he went to school, he pushed the bell.

Morris let him in quickly and shot off back to the telephone he was answering. As Mark stood in the hall, looking upwards and listening, he realised that for the moment, at any rate, he had been saved. The long, undisturbed shafts of sunlight that slanted down from each landing window and from the skylight of the top flat told him that the upstairs part of the house was empty.

It was funny, there was never any mistaking that feeling of emptiness; you could almost smell it. You knew before you had run round the corner into a deserted classroom and almost before you had rung the bell on an empty house's door you knew there was going to be no one inside. Morris was still down below and one or two of the other tenants might be in their rooms, of course, but if any of the Munday family or Tata had been up above there would be bound to have been some sort of noise. The sound of Evie's scales or their father's typewriter would have come slipping down the sunshaft, or cross-chat and laughter between Mrs Munday and Seb would have bounced backwards up the stairs. Mark would have been able to hear the twins chattering away like starlings or the noise of clattering dishes or of Tata's sewing-machine. The Mundays seldom remembered to shut doors or managed to do anything quietly.

At least it gave him a little time to think what to say when he did see his father. As Mark started upstairs, still wondering what Dr Barth might have said, he noticed that the doctor's door was ajar. Probably just gone out in a hurry to get himself some of those horrible little dark cigars which he smoked, Mark thought, and looked quickly down over his shoulder into the hall. For such a heavy man Dr Barth could move surprisingly lightly, as though the soles of his feet were as plump and cushioned as his hands. It was quite on the cards that he might creep in and be half-way up the stairs behind Mark before he noticed. But it was all right, there was still nobody down below.

Mark wondered for about the hundredth time why he disliked Dr Barth so much. It was something that neither he nor the rest of his family could understand. His father had given him one of his rare lectures about it once, telling him that Dr Barth was a very clever and kind man; and even his mother, who never interfered with anything that her children did, said what a funny boy he was to feel like that. Tata had pulled out some of her stock disapproving remarks about it and Seb had pointed out casually that there were lots of people in the world uglier than old Turkish Bath. And anyway, you couldn't go round hating people just because of the way they looked, he said, and because they'd had an accident to their finger once, long ago.

But it was all no good; Mark couldn't help himself. It was like hating porridge with lumps in, or herrings for breakfast; just a personal thing. However much Dr Barth's mouth smiled, the sight of the unsmiling black eyes above it made Mark's skin creep and the thought of being touched by those fat hands, and by that limp finger which hung down inside one of them, made him squirm. But oddest of all was this quite certain feeling he had that something was wrong. For all Dr Barth's smoothness and politeness Mark felt that he was watching all the time, like a cat waiting to pounce.

'But that's nonsense, old boy,' Mr Munday had said when Mark tried to explain this to him, at the end of the lecture about not being rude. 'Whatever should he want to pounce on? Dr Barth's been a very great help to me, though his line of country is a little different from mine.'

As Mark remembered the sound of his father's voice, saying this, he found he was outside the open door of the study. Thinking he would just have a little dip into the special feeling and a sniff at the good smell which always lingered there, Mark went in.

The room was shaped like an L and the desk was in the long part of it. Mark was round the door and well inside

before he saw that the room wasn't empty after all. Standing over the desk was Dr Barth.

Afterwards, when Mark tried to remember what had really happened, going over and over it all in his mind, he found he couldn't; it had all been too quick. And then, when everyone had talked so much, and disbelieved him, he got thoroughly confused. He only knew that when he first went into the room he could have sworn that the window was shut and that Dr Barth had moved quickly backwards to push it open. He was quite certain everything had been still when he first looked round the corner and then suddenly, all in a moment, there was this breeze coming in through the open window, like there had been on the lake, and the papers on the desk blowing about. As Dr Barth made as if to slap one or two of them down with his hand to stop them blowing off the table it seemed to Mark that he was holding on to one particular sheet and trying to fold it, to slip it away without being noticed. What on earth was he doing... what...

'It was so windy!' said Dr Barth, 'I saw that your father had left the door open and that some of the papers had blown on to the floor,' but as he was talking it seemed to Mark that his fingers were still plucking at the edge of this one sheet, trying to shuffle it away. Messing about with one of his father's papers, that belonged only to him!

'The window wasn't open!' Mark said suspiciously, 'I think it was you! And how could you see from downstairs, anyway? You shouldn't read it! It's my father's, it's private...'

'Now, Mark,' Dr Barth's politeness changed to something more unpleasant and a hiss like steam seemed to grow behind his smooth voice. 'What's this? I think you are forgetting you manners again, young man; as you did this morning. I had intended not to tell your father about it, but really, now...'

And still it seemed to Mark that under all this cover talk Dr Barth was trying to get the doubled-up sheet into his pocket. He mustn't! But as Mark tried to push forward across the table to stop him Dr Barth put out his other, horrible hand, like a fan with one spoke broken, the damaged finger dangling down.

'You're not to take it; put it down!' From out of the blur that covered it all afterwards Mark could only remember shouting and the awful feeling of desperation that he got as he tried to get past that hand. If only he could get some more strength from somewhere ... to hit it away ... he must save his father's paper ... he ...

As his determination grew he suddenly felt everything in him gather into one funny sort of arrow in the middle of his forehead again and he let fly. And at the moment that he pushed forward something swift and strong sprang with him.

Midway! Everything cleared and the glorious fact of him came back again. Mark never knew whether it was he who did it or the tiger or whether it was both of them acting together. But in one great leap there seemed to be a striped form on the desk top and with one great paw Dr Barth's hand was smacked away and he overbalanced on to the ground. Teeth tore the paper from him and a warm mouth pushed it into Mark's hand.

A chair crashed as the breath fanned Mark's cheek and then, before he could even speak to his tiger, he was gone. On the other side of the table Dr Barth had scrambled to his feet again and was staring at Mark. He moved a step or two towards him and then stopped as they heard the front door slam down below and the sound of Mr Munday's footsteps coming up the stairs.

'What...'

'Father!'

Mark remembered that his father had looked first at him and the torn sheet of paper and then at the Doctor, dishevelled and angry and very much the worse for wear.

'Father...'

But Dr Barth was bursting into speech now, and, because he was grown-up, he won.

'Hush, Mark,' Mr Munday held a hand up, 'Let Dr Barth speak. What's been going on?'

'This boy...' Shaking with rage Dr Barth pointed to Mark and the paper. 'I heard a noise, I came in... I saw what he was doing and then, when I tried to stop him, he was at me like a fury... like a tiger! With his teeth and his nails – look!' he pointed indignantly to a long red scratch on his hand and then to the sheet of writing in Mark's hand.

As Mark looked first at the torn paper and then at the sheets which had scattered on the floor; at the overturned chair and Dr Barth's appearance, with his tie loosened and his collar torn, he suddenly saw to his horror that it all added up.

'But it wasn't me!' he cried in despair. 'It was the wind – it was because of him ... he wanted to get this paper ... he opened the window so that they'd all blow!' But as he looked over towards the window he saw that somehow, in all the fracas, Dr Barth had managed to get it shut again.

His father looked at him.

'But why?' he said, rather helplessly, obviously not believing Mark, 'Why should you want to spoil my papers?' He said it gently, as though he were trying desperately to understand. 'You must know how long I've spent on them and what a short time there is to get them finished before the lecture. You know how important they are, to me and to us all...' He looked away from Mark and over to Dr Barth, puzzled and looking for an explanation.

Taking his cue from Mr Munday, Dr Barth stopped being angry and looked sad too. Sad! After what he had been doing! Mark could have hit him.

'It is well known, I am afraid,' Dr Barth said in his oiliest voice, shaking his head, 'that there is sometimes this jealousy, Mr Munday. So often in a middle son ... Perhaps Mark felt that you like these papers more than you like him; that they take up too much of your time, too much of your interest. I am afraid I shall have to tell you what he said to me only this morning; I had hoped that I needn't. I have tried to be patient and reasonable, but really, when he flew at me and knocked me down...'

'But I didn't; it wasn't me!' burst out Mark in despair, to his father. 'It was Midway, my tiger!' and the moment he had said it he knew somewhere deep down inside him that he had broken a rule.

'Mark,' said his father, 'I think you had better go upstairs.'

8

As Mark went away up the top flight of stairs, making himself go slowly to show that he wasn't afraid of Dr Barth, the silence from the open study door seemed to follow him like a thick beam. He knew that they were only waiting for him to be out of sight and hearing before they started discussing it all and for Dr Barth to tell his father about this morning, but apart from that he was in such a state of confusion that he hardly knew whether his feet were touching the stairs or not.

In one part of his mind he could still see Dr Barth's angry face and in spite of everything he grinned to himself as he thought of that satisfying smack; in another he saw his father's worried one. And yet all round him there was this wonderful thought that seemed like a bullet-proof jacket, protecting him from everything. Midway had come again! His friend, Midway, had come when he needed him! He wasn't alone any more.

Dazed as a sleep-walker he stepped up on to the top landing, and under the skylight the dusty brilliance of the evening sun dazzled him even more. Midway! The things that had happened to him since this morning that he had somehow forgotten about; to him, dull, ordinary Mark Munday! But he had certainly got himself into some trouble too.

He could hear various noises in the flat now; while he had been in the study the rest of the family must have come in. A slow, rather listless rattle of crockery from the kitchen sounded very unlike Tata's usual runaway-railway washing-up noises and Mark, who found that he was suddenly extremely hungry after all that had happened to him, went

across to see what was going on and if he could scrounge any scraps.

Instead of Tata he found Evie, perched on the stool with her long hair falling forward over her shoulders and practically into the sink, a flood of tears doing almost as much washing-up as the tap water.

Evie's hair was her personal sort of barometer. The higher her spirits the redder it became and when she was feeling low it sank down into something quite ordinary again. Today it was nearly brown and hung as limply as seaweed brought away from the sea, catching its own share of the copious tears.

At any other time Mark would have turned away quickly at such an embarrassing sight and gone off on his own, but now, for some reason, he felt different. In spite of the trouble hanging over his head the wonderful comforting thought of Midway was still all round him. Perhaps it was because of this or perhaps because of the large slice of bread and dripping which he'd found and was eating that he felt this sudden rush of sympathy for his sister; perhaps it was just because of his own troubles, but anyway he wanted to help.

'What ...' It was difficult to know what to say, because he wasn't in the habit, but Mark took a step forward and stood close beside her, hoping that perhaps some of his sympathy might spill out on to her, like heat from an electric fire. That was what dogs did when they knew you were in trouble, and that was what Jamie did too. It seemed to Mark to be the best way.

Holding a tea-cup up against her in surprise at seeing this unusual brother, Evie turned a blotchy face towards him.

'Is ...' said Mark shyly, 'Is it the music-master, Evie?'

She shook her head wildly so that a tear flew off and got quite round before it hit the draining board.

'Oh, him,' she said and then miserably pushed an open book towards Mark, pointing with one damp finger to an even damper page. 'Oh, Mark,' she said with a rush, 'It's awful, quite, quite awful because I'll never, never – it's someone who died a thousand years ago. It's Alexander!' and with her voice rising on the end of the word like a train wailing through a tunnel she jumped and rushed away to her room before a fresh storm of tears overtook her.

Mark stared down bewildered at the young man's pictured face. Alexander the Great. A history book: gosh, he was glad that he wasn't a girl! He cut himself another slice of bread and contact with such everyday things as the knife and the bread board brought him back from ... from ... whatever was it that he'd been thinking about that had been so exciting? Well, from the thought of Alexander, he supposed, and the thought of his own present troubles again.

Coming rows seemed to be able to give warning of themselves like thunderstorms and as Mark munched on he felt the atmosphere thickening all round him. He got up and started wandering restlessly from one room to another, waiting for the storm to break.

The flat was in a funny state anyway because it was only a week before the end of term. All last year's put-away holiday clothes had been got out again and strange objects like frog feet and snorkels, picnic sets and bird watching binoculars littered the chairs. Tata had been doing a big wash and there were piles of newly-ironed shorts and cotton skirts everywhere, with shrunken looking bathing things, peppered with moth holes in spite of her care. They must be moths' favourite food, Mark thought idly, picking up his to see how it had weathered the winter; perhaps they liked the salt in them, because he never remembered a year without holes.

As he was examining his shorts the washed twins came out of the bathroom on their way to bed, smelling hot and flannelly and soapy. They were extraordinary creatures, like the bits of paper that turn one colour for acid and another for alkali, and as if they knew instantly, without being told, that Mark was in trouble and ought to be avoided they threw him identically suspicious glances. Tata, bustling along behind them like a sheep-dog, followed their glances with one of her own, but hers was suspicious for purely practical reasons.

'Now you put that szwim suit down over there, Mark,' and she pointed to another pile of clothes, 'Is all ready for packing, you not to disturb!' It was the twins' pile she was pointing to; Mark could see the mackintosh gleam of rompers. So he was going away with them again.

For the summer holidays nowadays the family scattered in

various directions while their flat in Sicily Place was left empty, with dust sheets over all the furniture. In the old, good days before everything had got awkward for Mark, all of them used to go together to Wealdstowe, whose sand it was that now trickled out of Mark's bathing trunks on to the carpet. The Munday family filled and took possession of one small boarding-house and from the room that Mark always had he could see the simple, happy holiday pattern through the window; a stripe of sky, a stripe of sea and a stripe of sand below. If you moved up close to the glass you could make it four, for there was then a green stripe of the downs beneath you, leading away from the boarding house to the shore.

After the jumbled shapes of London it was most beautifully uncomplicated; the wind blew straight, with no buildings to hit up against and the sun came as straight down as the rain. Whichever you had – though the sun was obviously best, of course, it didn't really matter; Mark loved them all because they came from Wealdstowe. Wealdstowe sun, Wealdstowe wind and Wealdstowe rain; he would have liked to put them in three bottles and bring them home with him, to keep on his mantelpiece and sniff for all the rest of the year.

When the wind or the rain came too hard there was the small covered pier with slot machines; you could watch mechanical football games or see firemen jerkily rescue a burning lady; you could try to dredge up sweets with a pair of metal claws or stamp your name out on a strip of rose-coloured tin, like the one that was tacked outside Mark's door now. There were boats, fishermen and shops full of fishing things and everything was clean, windswept, sticky and smelling of salt. You tasted salt when you licked yourself, even if you hadn't been in the sea, and this seemed to Mark to be the true mark of holiday, the thing that made you know you were really there. That was Wealdstowe and once they were settled there each year the family quickly disposed of themselves on whichever of the stripes they liked best.

Down on the yellow stripe the twins gambolled decorously and beat spades about on the sand, while Tata screamed to them like a sea-gull when they got out of reach. Seb and Evie were more often to be seen doing advanced sort of swimming and diving in the mackerel-blue, white flecked stripe of the sea, while Mr and Mrs Munday would probably be far away where the green grass stripe met the sky, the one painting while the other walked and thought. When he came back Mark liked to see his father's hair blowing up in the wind, as though it were on holiday too, and his face, let out from the electric light of the study and the screwed-up wrinkles of concentration, growing smoothed-out and brown. It was holiday faces, like holiday clothes, that were right, he thought; working faces and town faces were wrong. At the very sight of Tata and his father with their seaside looks he felt happier at once, because then it seemed likely that they could last forever, but he never felt that he had to worry about his mother; she lived the whole of her life like a holiday, even when she was working, and always looked well.

Poking his finger through one specially large hole and still thinking about Wealdstowe, Mark sighed and finally put the shorts down. The last year or two everything had been different. His mother, pining for brighter colours, had gone abroad to paint and his father had stayed in London because he wanted to be nearer the library; Seb and Evie had taken to doing unsettlingly new things like going on canoeing holidays and camping away with friends. Last summer it had been only Mark, Tata and the twins who had gone off to the sea.

It had worked out fairly all right because Mark had his own friends there among the fishermen's tough children, who were like Jamie, but behind it there was always the same old problem, that he didn't quite fit in. Fishermen's children went back to fishermen's meal times and not to sandy sandwiches and when they bathed they jumped in swiftly from the break-water and not in a feeble, holiday-making sort of way from the beach. The sea was a business to them and not a pleasure and Mark felt rather ashamed that his family only came down to be swimming at its edges and not fishing right out in its deeps.

But this year, he thought more cheerfully, dimly beginning to remember something good, this year he'd go far off among the dunes to the lighthouse, take his picnic lunch with him and eat it lying stomach down in the warm white sand. There was a special hollow where the wind didn't blow stinging little pieces at you, where the grass stood up in stripy spears against the sky...

Stripes! The excitement that had been lurking at the back of his mind suddenly gathered itself together and he fully remembered again. Midway! How could he have ever forgotten! He shook his head violently, for it seemed to happen when his mind got full of other things. Could Midway come to Wealdstowe too? Would he come padding across the dunes with him, diving into the sea as he had dived into the lake beside Jamie, scooping a fish up with his majestic paw, reflecting the bright, sparkling sea water in his green lamps of eyes? Would Mark feel that fur again, smell it ... need he never feel dull or alone any more, ever again?

He shut his eyes for a moment, sniffing, and just as though he had been on the beach again he suddenly heard Tata's voice shrilling across the hall. He opened his eyes.

'Mark! You are to go to see your father now. Hooray!' She meant he was to go quickly for this was a word that Tata never got right.

So this was it. D-Day. Well, he didn't mind, he still had .... but as Mark's nervousness increased he seemed to forget everything again, even Wealdstowe. Brushing the holiday sand off his clothes, he hurried down towards the study.

9

MUCH later that night Mark woke up, but it wasn't like any of his usual wakings; it was in the pitch black dark.

At least it wasn't quite dark because there was a feeble little night light flickering away beside him, but it was darker than dark all round it and the curtains were drawn. His room had a stealthy, secret sort of look, as though he shouldn't really be seeing it in such an off moment as this. It seemed to be busy living its own life, and he guessed that it must be a time that he had never been awake before.

It was. Pulling his watch under the bedclothes, so that the luminous hands showed, Mark saw that it was two o'clock.

Two o'clock! Gosh! Two in the morning. And a night-light too. What had been going on? Mark sat up a little way and humped his knees. The night-light cheered up a little as though it were glad it had company and Mark, feeling quite wide awake now, stared at the dark screen of wall behind it.

He began to remember, and as though the wall were a cinema screen all the astonishing happenings of the day flickered across it. As Mark looked at the dark humping shadows of the furniture now he could hardly believe that it was the same room he had woken in that morning.

School and the museum seemed years and years away and Hayhoe and Riding and Professor Jellicoe seemed as remote as the statues there. Jamie ... Dr Barth ... but the doctor still seemed all too horribly near, and Mark hated the thought that he was asleep somewhere in this actual house. Evie in floods over her Alexander ... his father ... But all the time he was remembering these Mark was aware of something else in his mind, a feeling that there was something there waiting for him, like a wonderful birthday parcel, something so marvellous that he kept putting off the moment of taking it out. What could it be? He switched his thoughts back. Why was he awake now, in the middle of the night?

Mid ... Midway! But, of course, it was because of him. Now, in the darkness, with his mind quite empty, it seemed easy to remember. He had been thinking about his tiger, about having his wonderful tiger with him at Wealdstowe when Tata had called him to go downstairs to his father. That was it.

The very thought of that interview made Mark go hot all over and now he realised why all his sleeping time had gone funny and why he was sitting up here thinking, in the extraordinary middle of the night. He had babbled on so that they thought he had a temperature and had put him to bed early, with aspirins. But the aspirins had fought a losing battle against all the things he had to think about and had worked themselves out. Now he was wide awake again, and as he remembered his father's talking-to Mark shivered again, even after being so hot.

It had been dreadful. His father hadn't been cross, which would have been better, but had looked all sort of creased and worried, as though someone had crumpled his face up in their hand. Mark felt all the worse because he knew that his father was trying to get an important part of his work finished that week and that he ought to be left in peace.

But he hadn't done anything to be talked-to about! That was what made it so stupid! Except for the silly thing he'd said to Dr Barth that morning, and surely his father would understand about that? He had tried to explain, but like all Mark's explanations nowadays it only seemed to make things sound worse for he found that everything else came crowding in to get explained as well, the museum and the winged bulls; and Mr Bletchly suddenly saying that poem.

'And it just *was*...' Only then he remembered that he mustn't say anything about Midway. 'Well, of course I knew about the lamb, any clot would remember that, but I was so surprised! ...' And then about Jamie and the willow leaves but he had to stop short in the middle of those, and Dr Barth and...

'He *was* trying to steal that paper – I know he was!' but his father's face still didn't come out of its creases. He had drummed a bit on the table and then asked Mark if he had been finding the work at school too hard?

'...are they pushing you on a bit too fast, Mark? It should be all right for you, Seb was a form higher at the same age, but perhaps as you're growing ... Do the lessons bother you? Do you find that you can't quite keep up? Professor Jellicoe...'

Mark stared at him. There was this business about infinity, of course, and things like two negatives making a positive. But apart from them he could follow all right, as much as anyone ever could follow work. As well as Hayhoe, anyhow, he had better marks than him. Did his father really think that he'd gone off a bit? He couldn't!

'But Dr Barth was trying to take your paper! Really and truly he was!' Why wouldn't his father believe him? 'And I did know the answer to that question! I knew lots about the Assyrians too, in the museum, only it was Tiglath Pileezer, and Hayhoe tickling me! And – oh Father, I didn't mean it about you this morning ... I only didn't want him to know what I felt, I wanted to keep it...'

Looking out at the calm darkness now Mark supposed that it really must all have sounded a bit odd, especially as even after he had left his father's study he had gone on trying to make someone believe him about Dr Barth. He'd tried to tell his mother, tell Seb, even tell distracted Evie, and in the end they had said, 'There, there,' taken his temperature, given him these aspirins and pushed him off to bed. But just before he had gone off to sleep his father had come in again and sat down by his bedside; in the inky shadows Mark could still see the chair he had used and pushed back a bit and smell the cigar ash he had flicked into the night-light saucer.

'Well, don't worry, it'll be holidays soon, old boy,' he said, 'Do you know what we have decided to do? Your mother and I think you're getting a bit too old to go off to Wealdstowe with Tata and the twins ...' he leant back and inhaled a long draw from his cigar, 'How would you like to come down to Sussex with me?'

'With you? Just the two of us? Oh, yes!'

'I'll be dreadfully busy, I'm afraid,' Mr Munday was flattered at Mark's evident pleasure, 'You know I've only a week or two left now to get my work finished, so I'll tell you what we've arranged ... we're going to take a young man down there with us. He'll be a companion and can help you on with your lessons a bit for an hour or two a day, so you'll catch up for next term. He's a family friend of Dr Barth's ... who thinks he'll be just right for you. What was his name now?' He had taken a bit of paper from his pocket. 'Oh, yes; Clay, Eric Clay. You and he can do all sorts of interesting things together, so that you won't have any time for these ... fantasies,' and then he had ruffled Mark's hair as he said good night and switched off the light.

The aspirins had started to work by then and Mark was too sleepy to think much about it, but as he stared at the flickering shadows and considered the thought, how he wriggled in his bed. A friend of Dr Barth's! Someone called Eric Clay!

How really maddening it was to be a child, he thought for the hundredth-millionth time in his life, and have everything decided for you, without even being asked! It was like being some feeble sort of sea anemone, lying on the bottom of the sea, while everything that concerned you was happening somewhere up on the surface, miles above. 'You'll like that ... That'll be splendid, won't it? ... We've arranged ...' But they never asked you your opinion or waited to hear the answer and you never got a say in your own life.

The things they arranged were so stupid, too. Look at school, for instance – three-quarters of your year spent there and only one at home – about seven-eighths of your day indoors and only one out, as if those weren't crazy arrangements! And now look at Wealdstowe and all the plans he'd made for that summer. They made you get used to something and then, when you'd done so, they just picked you away from it like a limpet from a rock. They'd dangle something lovely in front of you, like summer holidays in Sussex with your father, and then poke in something extra which spoilt it all – a tutor! Mark didn't want a tutor, he was perfectly all right about next term's work; he just wanted to be alone to wait ... to wait for Midway. And at the word, at long last, forgetting all his annoyance, Mark really let himself press open the secret panel in his mind.

Midway; his tiger, his friend Midway. Because of him he wasn't ever going to be dull or alone, or insignificant any more. Mark and Midway – lovely, glorious, strong Midway! Remembering the island and wishing that the tiger were with him now Mark rolled over in the bed like a puppy, rubbed his face in the pillow and wrestled with the sheets, pretending they were fur. Then he pulled himself upright again and sat looking at the wavering night-light flame.

The trouble was that this new friend of his was rather like that flame himself. Sometimes he was strongly there, sometimes he wavered so that even the memory of him grew weak and sometimes he blew straight out. He came and went so quickly that there was never time to ask him anything, never time to talk...

How, *how* could he get him back again? 'Midway!' Mark tried once again, softly and beseechingly to the darkness and then waited. He felt the bed on either side of him, looked on the floor for an extra curled-up pool of blackness but there was nothing there. Rules, Midway had said; there were rules about it – but what rules ... how ... ? Mark tried to think, think only of the tiger and of what he had been doing on the island; in the study.

It made his head too sore; he wasn't used to such concentration. What with that and tossing about because of being awake in the middle of the night his forehead grew so hot that he slipped out of bed to rub it on the window glass, behind the curtains.

The moon was up now and as he stood there in his pyjamas with his face against the cool pane he could see clearly down into the empty street below.

How strange it was! Like the room, it was all secret and its own place now; if there had been any people they would have seemed like trespassers. You could hardly believe that it was the same Sicily Place as in the daytime when it was pavement-grey and dotted with many-coloured passers-by. Now it was black with yellow pools of lamplight and white streaks of moonlight and the cracks of sky between the houses were dark,velvet blue with yellow prickings of stars.

Stars. Mark lifted his forehead and looked up, so that now it was his chin which was rubbing on the glass. They seemed to be looking down at him. Perhaps he was the only person awake in the whole world, the only little black dot at a window they could see. He thought of them swivelling like silver searchlights all round the world, lighting up sleeping faces, shining on rivers ... on the sea. Of their light falling on the separate leaves of trees in great forests, glittering on the cold tops of mountains ... on the feathers and fur of all the animals curled up everywhere, fast asleep ... As Mark thought of them all his mind seemed to stretch away right out of himself and into the starlight and then he began to hear a humming and feel a thrumming, a sort of vibration as

though he and the sky and the streets were all shivering down the length of themselves . . .

There were narrower stripes in the street now than the moonlight ones and a darkness that was deeper than the velvet night. There was something which curved in a great leap through the air as the stars picked out everything shining white hair for an instant; then they were blotted from Mark's sight. He had only just time to step back from the window before the lithe form nearly knocked him over, then he was back by his bed again and rolling, scuffling, fighting and laughing as he had been doing in imagination only a few minutes before.

A little later, Mark lay breathless and laughing against the pillow and Midway, stretched out on the floor, was licking himself straight. Mark flicked himself over till he was lying face down and hung an arm over the edge of the bed to run his finger along the edge of Midway's spine.

'Midway,' he asked again, urgently. 'Why do you come and go so much? Why can't you be here always? *How* can I call? How ... why ... do you come?'

Midway stopped licking and his green eyes glinted briefly in the moonlight as he looked up.

'You call,' he said again, in that think-voice that was so warm and deep and comforting, but was now a little puzzled too. 'I can only come when you do. It's like someone hitting a gong with a special note ... a pulling, like being at the end of elastic ... well, and then I'm here.'

'But from where?' asked Mark again, 'And in the between whiles, while you're not with me, where do you go?' A really horrible thought was beginning to come to him, clouding his mind like drops of ink in clear water, 'You are all mine, aren't you? Nobody else can call?' As the bothers started to come in again he gazed down into the splendid eyes for reassurance and the most dreadful thing started to happen.

The moonlight stripes seemed to grow thin, then waver and melt away into nothing. Feeling the comfortable presence go from beneath him Mark rolled farther over again and reached out to try and hold Midway, but his hands closed on nothing. There was a warmth and a smell of grass in the room for a moment but then that too was gone and only the old dull smell of Mark's bedroom was left. Mark hauled himself up again, feeling the cold iron edges of the bed. He'd sent Midway away again! Whatever had he done?

The aspirins must have still have had some kick in them after all for after a while of half-pleading and half being angry, of padding backwards and forwards to the window and looking up at the stars; of calling ... beseeching ... Mark fell asleep.

IO

FOR the next few days after that Mark's life went into a sort of blur. It was like those times at Wealdstowe when a bank of mist would roll in from the sea and cover everything in cotton wool, so that the most ordinary landmarks looked like something from a dream world and he just couldn't think clearly at all.

His parents, still treating him like a semi-invalid, had decided that he needn't go back to school again, 'for I gather that you haven't any prizes to collect,' Mr Munday had said rather wryly. Prizes! Who cared about those! If only they knew what had really happened to him! Mark was still dazzled by the glory and the sorrow of it.

Sports day had been earlier in the term, so he didn't mind missing school in the very least. The only sad thing was that it would have been so splendid, so absolutely splendid, if he could have felt Midway come bounding along beside him in the park, if he could have gone swaggering into school knowing that he was there too. Not that anyone else would have seen him, of course, Mark realised that now, but it was just that if Midway had been there he knew he would have felt twice the person that he normally was. If he could have had him sitting there beside his desk, reaching down every now and again to feel the deep fur, how little he would have cared for Riding or Hayhoe or anything they could do!

But the trouble was that you never knew whether Midway would come or not. It was just like everything else in life, Mark thought disappointedly, like playing games or learning to swim or skate. At first it had seemed as though it would be so gloriously, effortlessly easy to get him and now there seemed to be all these invisible rules about things to do and not to do. He mustn't talk about Midway and he mustn't...

Mark tried to go over in his mind every thought, every word he had used on the island yesterday, in the study, in the moonlight. But his tiger was gone now, so completely gone that there were moments when even Mark himself began to wonder if he hadn't been dreaming, if it wasn't just a memory left over from the museum, all mixed up with aspirins and things. But then he remembered the willow island, the paw that had slapped at Dr Barth in his father's study; and the dark shape leaping in at the moonlit window and he knew that Midway was true.

But why was he called Midway? Each time Mark meant to ask that. And where, oh where, did the tiger go when he went away? As he tried to imagine it, pictures of places that were as strange as the midnight mountain tops came flickering into his mind, pictures made from all the bits of poetry he had ever heard, the films he had seen and the illustrations in his explorers' books: from Seb's stories, his mother's paintings and even old Tata's fairy books. He began to dream of shadowy caves and far-off mountain ranges, deserts whose sand was as tawny-coloured as the tiger's own fur. But the more Mark puzzled about it all and the more far-away the look in his eyes grew, the more unnaturally his family treated him, as though he were sickening for something.

It was funny to be home at the wrong time of year and horrid to be thought slightly ill and Mark wandered about from one person to another, among all the piles of packing that were still lying about, trying to explain to them that he was really perfectly all right and to reassure himself by asking them what they thought that his tutor was going to be like. Sometimes he felt rather grand to think that he was going to have such a person to himself and at others he felt extremely cross that they weren't going to leave him to be alone with his father. These grown-up arrangements! The worst aspect of the whole thing, to his mind, was that this Eric Clay had been chosen by Dr Barth.

'What do I think he'll be like? Oh, gorgeous, probably!' said Evie with a great sigh, for the strain of loving someone as hopelessly far ago as Alexander was beginning to tell.

'Difficult to say,' said Seb, out of a mouth full of drawing pins and in the darkness of his projector room, 'The Eric part's all right, sort of sharp and noble, but Clay sounds as though he were a little mannikin moulded specially by old Turkish Bath to annoy you.' They were not much help.

Tata, sometimes falling in with the invalid idea and sometimes remaining her usual self, alternately either fed Mark indulgently on all the spare knobs and edges of whatever she had been baking or gave him lectures about how to look after his holiday clothes on his own, while the twins, once again catching the general atmosphere like two little bits of blotting paper, rubbed up against Mark like kittens and kept offering him their best toys to play with. His mother, acting on her belief that the best cure for having anything wrong with you was to do something totally different and violently active, made him pose for her as a 'boy running' and kept him hopping from one leg to another for what seemed to him like hours.

The studio was a strange place, in which all his mother's ideas seemed to have taken on a vivid life and for one wild moment, as he stood there on tiptoe amongst the brilliant and living splashes, Mark felt a terrible urge to tell her about Midway and to ask her how you made things come true. But he wasn't used to talking to her and although he tried to get the words straight in his mind, they wouldn't come out.

All in all, it was quite a relief when Sunday, the day to go down to Sussex, came. The thought of going off alone with his father, like two men together, and starting the holidays before the others did, was very exciting, but behind it there was always the pricklingly tiresome thought of this Eric Clay.

The morning dragged on till lunch, but then at last that was over and their suitcases and the big box full of his father's books were stowed away in the boot of the car. Odd coats, shoes and all the things that Mark kept running off to fetch thinking he might need them, filled up the cracks. The lid was slammed down and locked and then they were ready at last and there were the rest of the family and Tata lined up by the door. Pecking at his mother's cheek and waving to the rest Mark slid on to the warm leather of the seat beside his father.

'All ready? Brought everything you want? Good heavens, I should think you have. All right then, we're off.'

The big and powerful old car, somehow so very suitable for Mark's father, slid away down Sicily Place. Mark looked shyly from the polished wood of the dashboard to the holiday tweed of his father's sleeve; up from the strong hands on the wheel to his father's profile, and a great wash of joy splashed over him, as warm as the sun which was already pouring in through the windscreen. He caught his father's eye in the driving mirror and they both grinned.

His father was in holiday mood too and suddenly, for the first time for ages, everything came easy between them, like a key turning in a well-oiled lock. They talked and made jokes about the passing cars and drivers, while Mark watched out for the traffic lights and read the map. Deputising for his father he scowled at offending drivers and acknowledged the courtesies of obliging ones with a regal flip of his hand, imagining that his father was a super-important V.I.P. whom he was officially guiding through London. He was doing it just as well as Seb could, he thought; if only it could always stay like this!

They sailed down the wide streets of the West End and crossed the river; correctly guided by Mark they triumphantly joined the circular road that was to lead them out of London. This wound through narrower streets now and past terraces of shops, cinemas and little parks; all joined-together the villages that London really is. After a large church, a funny-looking red brick affair, very highly ornamented, Mr Munday swung out of the south-going stream.

'Right by the red brick church,' he said, 'and then second left. Well, you couldn't have a redder or a bricker church than that. Wellingborough Terrace: that's where we've got to pick up Clay.'

This was it. Although the sun was as bright as ever Mark's spirits fell and a shadow came over the day. As they drove into Wellingborough Terrace he looked at it with suspicion, the houses were dull and all alike, as though they had been built out of a set of nursery bricks, and he felt that only a dull person could come out of them. No. 9. They had drawn up outside and Mr Munday put his hand to the horn, but there was no need to press it for there was Eric Clay ready and waiting at the gate.

Readiness and eagerness seemed to be the keynotes of Mark's new tutor. Like a large, ungainly puppy he came bounding out of the gate with his pale eyes shining and his mouth already open, so as to waste no time in greeting them. His one free hand was hanging loosely at the ready, as though only waited to swing forward and clasp theirs, and long before the actual handshake Mark knew with a sinking feeling just what it was going to be like: one of those crushing and hearty affairs that left all your fingers squashed together for minutes afterwards.

'Good morning, sir!' After the pumping handshake he smiled brightly at Mr Munday and added to his greeting of Mark a conspiratorial wink.

'Ah, yes, Clay: very glad you were able to come at such short notice,' said Mr Munday, apparently not disconcerted, and as Mark got out, reluctantly realising he'd have to go in the back now, Eric Clay gave him a little clasp on the shoulder and then climbed clumsily in.

Mr Munday started off again and Eric Clay, evidently anxious to please and realising that he shouldn't talk while they were weaving their way on to the main road again, kept a bouncy silence, looking round every now and again to beam at Mark.

In between whiles, frowning slightly, Mark took stock.

He had to admit that he was baffled. Inside him, though he had never talked about it to anyone else, he seemed to have a funny thing, a sort of geiger counter about people. It was that which made him know that Mr Bletchly was all right, in spite of his wobbly appearance, and that Dr Barth was all wrong. It had spoken up once about a doorman they had and, sure enough, he had turned out to be a crook and had to go, but about Eric Clay it didn't seem able to give judgment at all.

'That's right, sir – fork left here...' Mark scrutinised his tutor's half-turned profile. The eyeballs were so prominent that you could almost see through them and the very short hair was so fine that Eric Clay's head looked like a baby's hair-brush.

That was the trouble, there was something pathetic about this chap. It was annoying; Mark could have worked up a good old lusty hate for all that bounciness, if all these funny soft bits hadn't kept getting in the way. He wondered what Seb would have made of him and giggled when he thought of Evie. His new tutor certainly wasn't an Alexander.

But soon Mark gave it up as a bad job. He'd find out soon enough and in the meantime it was just too boring to spend all his time wondering about Eric Clay. He'd never been out of this side of London before and he wanted to watch what was going on; as always in the last few days he wanted to go on thinking too; thinking about Midway. As they joined the main road again and direction problems were temporarily over, the new tutor started to talk to Mr Munday. Mark, letting the map sink down into his lap, leant back to look out of the window as they bowled along.

The green bits to either side of the road grew from gardens to small fields and then stretched themselves out even wider; sheds gave way to barns and people grew scarcer till they were outnumbered by cows. A field full of tall poles suddenly fled past them, with a sort of rigging of strings tied from one to another, and the pattern changed swiftly as they drove by, like harp strings, or some fascinating game in geometry.

'Hops!' said Mr Munday. 'Look, Mark,' and as Mark looked with interest he saw the thick plants beginning to trail up the strings, four to a post, as though gorillas were twining hairy green arms round them. He remembered Jamie and wondered if he might be somewhere down here, in the same part of the country?

'Yes, hops,' echoed Eric Clay, turning round with one of his sickly smiles, but then he turned back to Mr Munday and went on asking questions about his work. Would his father mind, Mark wondered; usually he hated talking about his special subject to anyone and it seemed jolly good cheek for Clay to be doing it now, but then he lost interest as the countryside claimed his attention again.

It was completely different from London, of course, and different from Wealdstowe too. It was much more hilly, and instead of the simple seashore pattern all the outlines here were lush and woolly with growing things till it looked as though someone had been doodling with a giant green pen. Grasses waved against the sky from the nearby banks and long trails of green wavered out from the hedges; the trees were great blocks of dark green shade and the fields were furred with silky rippling corn and silvery grass.

Furred ... rippling ... A happy feeling began to come over Mark.

'Which way now, Mark?' His father, happily confident of getting the right answer, tossed the question back, but Mark was miles away among waving corn ... on an island with willows ... in a moonlit street ...

'Midway ...' he began happily, and then coming back into the present again abruptly, 'Oh sorry, no! I mean ... Right, I think.' He dropped the map as he tried to get it open at the right fold and it took on a horrible flapping life of its own, like a stiff sail in a breeze. 'No, it isn't ... oh, bother!' and like all people caught napping when they are supposed to be map reading, he panicked and lost his nerve.

With a slur of brakes and signalling quickly, Mr Munday drew into the side. He had to wait while the stream of outraged cars behind him passed and then patiently reached over to take the map himself.

'The middle way,' he said patiently, 'would have landed us straight in the Saloon Bar,' for there was an inn, The Hop Pole, ahead of them, with the road forking to either side. 'Left. Perhaps you'd take the map now, Clay? Look, that's where we want to get ...' and Mark's new-found confidence collapsed.

'You see?' his father's glance seemed to be saying to Eric Clay, and Mark felt his stock rushing downhill. He was no longer his father's helper and map reader, as Seb might have been. He had failed; he was just a stupid boy who needed a tutor in the holidays; dull, middle Mark again. As it always did, the feeling seemed to tie a lead weight on his tongue and bathe his brains in glue; although he knew his father was disappointed he couldn't even say the right sort of pleased things when they stopped in a village for late tea or when they drew up at the oast-house and were introduced to Farmer and Mrs Tompsett, who were letting them the rooms.

11

WAKING next morning in his strange round bedroom, Mark tried to collect up all his blurred memories and get them sorted in his mind. There had been a great flurry, he remembered, as they had all got out of the car and unpacked their suitcases from it and everything had been made much more complicated by Eric Clay's jolly efforts to help. Mark could still see his long, loose arms flailing around like windmill sails, picking up cases, coats, shoes and books which everyone else had just put down, always managing to get them all in the wrong places and in everybody's way.

There had been Mr and Mrs Tompsett, red-faced and friendly and like Noah's Ark farmers; a smell of country and apples and this sleepiness that made everything merge together for Mark in a wavering, under-sea sort of way. There must have been about three large black-and-white sheepdogs, suspicious at first but rapidly accepting the newcomers, for Mark remembered wagging tails and licking tongues and then a series of vague stripy cats who wove themselves in and out and among everyone's legs so that you nearly fell over them as well as over Eric's misplaced suitcases. While all the introductions were going on the late evening sunlight had been flickering down through the tall trees outside and when they went into the house there was all the dusty warmth of the day's stored-up hotness waiting for them.

The first thing Mark had noticed in the living-room was a table laid with goodly, Red-Riding-Hood sort of food; butter and a crusty loaf and a jugful of cream. Then he could only remember the sleep coming down over him thicker and thicker as he tried to eat his way through it all but failed. There was the funny sound of Eric Clay talking away to his father, a comfortable bumble of slow, deep country voices behind it; the sharp little face of some child or other peeping at him round a corner and instantly disappearing. Then the red tiles of the floor and the wide treads of the funny twisting stairs as, half-out on his feet, he was part-shown and part-pushed into his white and turrety room. Now, with the sun slanting in through the small window, he sat up in bed and took stock.

It was nice; he liked it. To have a round room was like being in a private fortified tower and as he thought some more about yesterday he felt he was going to need somewhere private to retreat. That Eric Clay! Oh, golly – was that his voice he could hear calling now? Mark looked at his watch and saw that it was nine o'clock.

Breakfast, he supposed, and jumping out of bed he shook himself into some sort of shape. Holiday clothes were quick and easy to put on and thank goodness there was no Tata to peer down his neck. Earnest though he was, he scarcely thought that Eric Clay would do that. When Mark got downstairs he found to his alarm that his father had already breakfasted and was at work in his study; he had to face his tutor across the table alone.

Mark said good morning and sat down, then, as he poured cream on to his cornflakes he stole a swift glance again at Eric Clay. He looked even worse this morning, Mark decided, in a blue shirt with a too-wide, open collar which made him look as though he were in a sailor suit. He was all on the bounce still, like a ball which had been thrown down and hadn't quite stopped moving, and he too was watching Mark, brightly and alertly, as though determined to get on good terms with his new pupil and make friends.

'Well, old chap, had a good night?' he said. 'This is a bit of all right, isn't it?' and as he waved towards the great dish of eggs and bacon, the yellow butter and the cream Mark had a sudden odd little twitch of sympathetic feeling inside him, an idea that the tutor's own breakfast table at Wellingborough Terrace wasn't usually loaded like this. He nodded, crunching up his cornflakes as the voice went bubbling on.

'I'm told we're to use this as our schoolroom – after the meals have been cleared, that is – your father suggests two hours' lessons a day ... Mornings, shall we say, and get it over with?' He laughed rather forcedly. 'Hard luck having a chap like me wished on you in the holidays! Never mind, we'll soon get used to each other and I dare say we'll have some good rambles together in the afternoons ...'

Rambles! Mark stiffened with horror, his spoon in mid-air. Would he have to go on being jolly with this chap all through the day, as well as during the horrible lesson hours? Wasn't he ever going to be alone? He must be! It was terribly important. Because there was Midway ... A dreadful picture sprang into Mark's mind of him and Eric Clay trotting through the fields and woodlands together, burbling on about spurgeons and hawk's tooth and whatever all those silly yellow flowers were called; about greater and lesser thises and thats and what sized eggs they laid.

Mark was no naturalist but he was observant about people. As he stared vaguely at the middle of Eric Clay's chest, so as to avoid the palely beaming eyes above it, he noticed that there were one or two burrs caught in the baby blue Aertex of his shirt. It looked as though he had been pushing his way through the undergrowth already and as his tutor lifted the cream jug Mark saw that there was a bramble scratch on the back of his hand. Going back to his cornflakes again he accidentally knocked his knife off the table and as he bent down to pick it up he noticed that there was mud on Eric Clay's dark-blue canvas shoes as well. Goodness! He'd been out for a walk before breakfast! Mark hoped that he wasn't going to be expected to join in those.

Eric Clay was still beaming at him and Mark knew that he ought to make some bright remark. It was one of those times when he longed to be Seb, who always found it easy to know what to say. But what sort of thing could you say to people like this – and what would he call this tutor anyway? Oh, well – here goes, he'd better try, he thought.

'Have you been out already, sir ... Mr ... ?' He mumbled the end of the sentence into a spoonful of cornflakes and then put it into his mouth so that nothing further in the way of chat could be expected of him.

'Oh, call me Eric, Mark. I'm not all that old or alarming, you know!'

Oh, gosh, that was the most embarrassing solution of all. But as Mark shot his tutor a glance he saw to his astonishment that Eric seemed to be feeling awkward at the question too for his pink face had become red and his plump chest heaved as he drew in a quick breath.

'Been out before breakfast? Good gracious no!' and he gave his little laugh. We don't do things like that, he seemed to be implying, as though he were trying to meet Mark on his own ground. Mark's geiger counter flickered wildly, like a compass whose needle was madly seeking north.

What was going on? Why on earth should Eric bother to tell a lie about something which didn't matter in the least? Because he had been out, it was quite obvious that he had. The shoes he wore yesterday had been leather ones and the pale-blue shirt was a newly-ironed and clean one – there was still a crease down the middle of it. Mark had seen an anxious-looking mother hovering about in the background of Wellingborough Terrace and he'd bet that she wasn't the sort to pack a shirt with burrs on, or shoes streaked with wet mud. But what on earth did it matter if Eric Clay did like going out in the early morning? Mark stared at his tutor in unconcealed surprise.

To cover up the awkward moment Eric started talking again, asking Mark so many questions, and so fast, that he felt like ducking as they all came shooting out at him like corks from a pop-gun. What did he like doing? (This dreadful grown-up question!) Who were his friends ... what did he find most difficult at school ... wasn't he proud to have such a famous father ... (Mark eyed him quickly and with embarrassment) and then, as Mark's answers, punctuated by breakfast, were not very forthcoming, Eric Clay gave up and went back to this tiresome and obviously favourite subject of rambles again, but luckily burbling on without expecting an answer.

It seemed that he belonged to a hiker's club in London and that every Sunday they used to put on their stumping great boots and go jollily out of town, singing and cracking jokes and swinging their sticks at hedges and thistle heads ('... must help the farmers when you can, you know.') getting themselves chased by bulls, and hung up on barbed wire; getting footsore and thirsty, but apparently happy, till the herd of them came thundering out of the train and on to the London platform again. Mark could just see them, shorts and ballooning anoraks and knobbly knees, and with this funny double feeling that he had for Eric, which seemed to be half distaste and half being sorry for him, he could see his tutor making his bouncy way back to the little house in Wellingborough Terrace, being greeted by his mother, fed on hot soup and presenting her with all the little bits of hawkstoe and pifflewort he had gathered during the day.

'But all the paths we take are well mapped out, of course; lots of chaps know about *them* ...' the voice was bubbling on, '... what I thought we'd do, Mark, old chap, this holiday, would be to get off the beaten track altogether and blaze our own trail across this part of the country, don't you think? We'll keep a record of it all. And on wet days we could make a map of it, you know ... cherubs blowing wind ... "Here be dragons" – that sort of thing, you know, to make it more amusing ... I expect you're good at drawing, what with your mother's talent. Not that a drop of rain will stop us walking,

of course!' He gave a great hearty laugh, 'We'll have good fun in that too, I'm sure ...'

Once again Mark found himself gazing at Eric in horror. Like walking in the rain! He must be bonkers. Listening to his voice was like being rained on; it was worse, it was like being hit on the head with a spoon; it went on and on and on. Walking! Another picture was growing up in his mind now, of himself in a bulging wind-cheater too, staggering after this non-stop talker 'thorough bush, thorough briar'. The words, which he had always thought particularly unattractive, suddenly floated into his mind.

And then suddenly, perhaps because the first part of his breakfast was starting to digest and glow comfortably inside him as he slowed down to the toast and honey stage, he saw the funny side of it. Earnest Eric crashing along through the countryside and earnest Mark trotting along beside him! What a holiday! He tried to think what Riding and Hayhoe might be doing and imagined himself telling them about this! 'Thorough bush, thorough briar ... *thorough mud ...*'

'*Thorough mire!*' He heard a rich, warm, lazy voice from beside him, 'Come on, let's put an end to this!' and Mark, his eyes lighting with incredulous joy, quickly put down his cup. Midway! Midway had come without Mark even knowing that he had called him!

'Oh, I never walk,' he said lightly, 'I always go everywhere on tiger back, I'm afraid,' and then, as radiant with joy as Evie would have been had she met her Alexander, he felt down with his hand to his side.

The effect of his words on Eric was instant and startling. As though someone had thrown a cloth over him he stopped dead in his flow of chat about rambling, looked at Mark with eyes full of concern and half put out a hand as though he would like to pat him and say 'there, there!' His thoughts were almost visible. This was the situation, he was obviously thinking, that he had been hired to deal with. But equally obviously he hadn't expected it to crop up quite so soon.

Giggling to himself inwardly Mark could almost see Eric saying to himself that he must be on his toes at once to deal with this, be tactful; jolly the boy out of it.

'But Mark, old chap, this is just your imagination, there aren't really those sort of tigers, you know.'

'No?' said Mark indifferently, but his hand by the chair was holding firmly on to something. As Mark went through the motions of stroking what seemed to be a large, non-existent animal Eric, who was watching, was almost dancing in his impatience to convince him that there was nothing there.

'We'll start our lessons,' he said eventually, and seemed happier when he could see both of Mark's hands on the table.

'I expect you were just trying out a joke on me, weren't you?' He felt he had sorted that one out and felt better. He must show he had a sense of humour! 'Now let's take this page here ...' but he saw that as Mark turned over the page, the boy's lips were moving.

'If you wouldn't mind just lying down, Midway,' he was whispering, apparently to the ground, 'and wait till I've finished these lessons?'

Eric Clay clucked and gritted his teeth.

'Now, what is the common denominator ...' and as Mark grudgingly bent his mind to the problem he slipped one hand down beside him again.

'Now, Mark, leave that dog ... that ti ... oh!' Eric blinked his pale eyes and flushed with distress.

'My tiger, do you mean? Oh, it's quite all right, Eric,' said Mark, bringing his hand up for the last time and smiling an angelic smile. 'He really doesn't like it much indoors and he can't stand common denominators anyway.' He looked over to the window. 'He's gone.

'... on a ramble,' he concluded, on the spur of the moment, and was sure that he heard a deep, quick chuckle from outside.

But he went on looking out reflectively. So that was another way, he thought in surprise, Midway could come when he laughed about things, as well.

12

ARITHMETIC – what a horrible, scratchy word for a horrible subject! Like a lot of other things, thought Mark, if it had been given a pleasanter name it might have been a better thing. Like himself, in fact. But as it was it sounded as stiff and knobbly as poor Tata's arthritis and the very word put you off before you'd even begun. And then it reminded Mark of something else and another unpleasant picture came into his mind which he as quickly tried to put out again. Dr Barth was quite bad and quite worrying enough in London, or wherever he was having his holiday, which Mark hoped was far away without bringing the thought of him down here.

None of these jumping thoughts, of course, helped very much with his concentration or provided him with anything but wildly guessing answers, but a fat lot he cared. At the back of his mind he knew that Midway was still waiting for him, somewhere beyond where the bright sun was shining down outside the oast-house, that as soon as he was out his wonderful creature would be there to meet him. Where would they go together and what would they do? A long shiver of excitement ran through Mark as he hopefully put down a bunch of figures that he thought might do.

'No, Mark!' exclaimed Eric Clay for the sixth or seventh time, trying to be patient but tapping the table nervously. 'The answer is 3·6 recurring – work it out!' But as Mark tried to juggle with the figures, which kept popping in and out of his mind's fingers like a lot of slippery different coloured balls, he saw that his tutor's eyes kept straying anxiously to the ground by his side. He grinned.

Lessons came to an end at last and all through lunch, brought in to them blessedly early by a beaming Mrs Tompsett, the tutor kept the conversation on a strictly hearty plane, determined to let in no thought or mention of a tiger. In the end it was Mark who was fidgeting with impatience. When was this going to stop? Surely he'd been in for two hours and more and surely they wouldn't go on after lunch? The sun was shining outside and the long summer afternoon was wasting, his entire thoughts were concentrated on how he could manage to get out and away on his own.

The problem was suddenly solved for him. Just as he had put in his second wedge of Mrs Tompsett's apple tart and had decided regretfully that, even as a platform for more cream, he couldn't manage another, the door opened and his father came in.

Mark spluttered and went scarlet and the tart stopped tasting good. Oh, dear, why did it always have to happen that when his father came in his mouth was stuffed with food? But this time, as Mark could see instantly, it didn't really matter, for his father was in his concentrating mood. It was a funny state, which turned him from a father into a stranger, a sort of Rip van Winkle traveller who seemed to have arrived back after years in a far away land and hardly recognised any of the everyday things he saw. He even looked different too. As large and splendid as ever, of course, and as goodly and nice smelling, but because of his far-away expression he looked even more like a statue, the sort that stare away into the distance so that you can never catch their eyes. Bringing this far-away gaze back with difficulty Max Munday looked first at the quite ordinary sugar sifter as curiously as though it were some rare carved chessman, then down at his son.

'Been indoors all this lovely morning?' he asked in surprise, looking at the pushed-back books and quite forgetting that it was he who had arranged that this should happen. 'You'd better get out, Mark, get some fresh air while you can. Clay . . . I wonder if you could help me with some checking? My other son, Sebastian, usually gives me a hand with it when I'm at home, but . . .' and though the usual twitch of shame plucked somewhere inside Mark he seized his chance before anyone could change their mind or mention rambles and slipped quickly through the heavy door and out into the sunshine.

He hurried down a path bordered by hedges, turned a corner and went on through a multi-coloured, multi-smelling flower garden till he found himself where the proper farm began, which interested him much more. He slowed down, drew in a long breath and took stock. For the first time since

Eric Clay had come bubbling into his life yesterday he was really able to look round and get his bearings. He stood quite still for a minute, next to a bush of flowers that was buzzing with bees and smelt like honey and thought how extraordinary everything had suddenly become.

First of all, behind and beyond everything, there was the glory of Midway. And as if that weren't astonishing enough in itself the whole of the rest of his life seemed suddenly to have altered too. Like being in this completely new place with his father instead of at Wealdstowe, like suddenly finding old bumbling Eric attached to him. As the bees buzzed all round him Mark thought for a moment of some of the even odder things that buzzed at the back of his thoughts and worried him, the memory of Dr Barth in his father's study and this mysterious early ramble of Eric's this morning. But oh bother them! He had better things than that to think of; he looked back along the way he had come.

This oast-house was a good sort of place to live in, he decided, it had a cosy, settled, no-nonsense look about it which he liked very much. Outside, the odd round rooms were still topped by their white cones, although, according to the lecture about oast-houses which Eric had given him at lunch time, the oast wasn't used for its original purpose of drying hops any more. The two white wind vanes sticking out from the tops of the cones gave the house a perky look, like someone waving, or with feathers in their hat. Beneath one of them he identified the window of his own top room, looking over the farm towards the distant woods, and saw Eric Clay's window below it. The other roundel, as Clay had told him they were called, belonged entirely to his father, with his bedroom above and a study beneath.

Behind them both ran the low red-brick room which was dining-room, sitting-room and schoolroom too, crouched like a nice long dog, like a lion, like ... Mark hugged his arms round himself and did a small hopping dance in the sunshine as he thought of his – oh, he was almost too splendid to be called a friend!

Four times now Midway had come; he counted them on his fingers; once on the island, once in his father's study, once in the moonlight and now here in the oast-house, this very morning. That was specially good because it meant that Midway didn't belong only to London, but could come here too; could come anywhere perhaps ... anywhere at all.

But how? When and how? The question still teased at Mark's mind. Midway said that he could only come when Mark called. But when he did call, and nearly burst himself with the strongness of his calling too, nothing happened at all. It seemed to be something to do with how he was feeling; the sort of mood he was in, but how in the world could you do anything about that? Moods just came, like the weather, and you couldn't make yourself laugh or do anything else at things if you didn't feel that way.

Mark tried to remember all over again what it had been like each time that Midway had come but his mind got so twisted up with thinking that he had to give it up. Perhaps it was like that teasing thing about not thinking about piebald ponies' tails and he should try to stop thinking about it at all? 'O Midway, come again!' he cried inside himself and made a determined effort to put his attention on something else.

What sort of a place had he come to? He started off again in the sunshine, more slowly now that he was well away from the house and safe from Eric, stopping occasionally to look back along the direction from which he had come. The farmhouse itself was at a little distance from the oast but its bricks were of the same warm colour and it had the same friendly, worn look of something very much used. Mark could see yesterday's cats sitting plumped out on its window-sills and one of the black and white dogs rubbing itself slowly backwards and forwards against a door-post. Like a shower of white flakes some fan-tail pigeons fluttered on to the red roof to sun themselves and he watched some other sort of little birds, brown and busy, going fussily in and out between the eaves.

Looking down from them Mark saw the kitchen cloths that had been put out to dry on the bushes round the back door and the cheerful-looking washing that flapped familiarly over the yard. He picked out the farmer's large shirts and a couple of brightly-flowered aprons that must belong to Mrs Tompsett; there was a skimpy looking cotton dress hanging beside them and then a succession of jeans, smaller and smaller as they tailed away down the line. It looked from that as though the Tompsetts had about six kids, but most of them too small sized for him, Mark guessed.

He pictured them round the farm-house too, using the inside just as familiarly as the animals were using the out. He felt that even the spiders on the beams inside the house and the little caterpillars that he had seen hunching their way up the warm bricks, the butterflies that quivered on the sunny sills, must have each staked out their own place where no one would disturb them and they could feel at home. It was different in London where everything got swept up and tidied and moved about so much.

The garden was as friendly as the house; it smelt nice and Mark moved on again, sniffing at the straggling roses, till he reached the roughly-clipped hedge beyond which the fields started. Some were of corn and there were some short, stubbly green ones where the hay had been cut; some were coverd in rich pasture where the cows were standing in bunches together and using all their tails in a sort of communal fan against flies.

Beyond these last fields rose the woods, covering the slopes of the hills and disappearing over their edge, only to appear again, bluer and fainter, like someone walking away into the distance, until in the end they were so pale in the heat bloom that it was difficult to tell which were woods and which was sky. It was Forestry Land Eric had also told him in their instructive lunch-time chat, and the farmers had to watch it very carefully for fires in this sort of weather. As Mark gazed at the grey-green expanse of leaf and needle shimmering silkily away into the distance, his mind stretched away with it too.

It was like 'the forests of the night' he thought, and as he lifted the latch of the little gate that led out into the fields and felt the sun-warmed metal hot under his palm another little latch seemed to click open and lead his thoughts away into strange, far-off places. Forest. It was a good word, deep and dark and exciting. Exciting as thinking about Midway was ... oh, goodness, but he'd had enough of thinking! He wanted to have him here, to be running with him, to be racing through the trees and think-talking to him ...

'*Tiger, tiger* ...' Mark screwed up his eyes and his thoughts. 'Midway, Midway ... *burning bright* ...' Was he coming? Yes, surely, for the air seemed starting to vibrate in that funny way again as though it was tightening; Mark's cheeks were beginning to burn and surely he could feel something tickling ... ? Slowly, hopefully, he opened his eyes but it was only the long grass, brushing against his knees. He hit at it angrily and knew instantly that he had done something wrong again. Midway had been very near, he knew he had, but now, for some stupid reason that he didn't understand the afternoon had turned back into an ordinary one again with nobody in it.

Oh, goodness it was difficult! The slightest wrong thought, the faintest bit of cross feeling and Midway went; it was like turning the knob of the radio and hearing snatches of sound but never quite getting on the right wave!

Mark looked round him and suddenly felt depressed. All at once he had got a picture of the wireless in the old schoolroom at home, with Seb and Evie arguing over the programmes they wanted and it made him feel homesick and alone. He stared round. He couldn't see any roads or cars and there were none of the farmer's men in sight, only the great empty bowl of the fields and the woods beyond. Instead of the familiar hum of London, friendly with cars and bus drivers, their was only a high, shrill buzz of insects, behind it a silence so strong that it seemed to echo like a clap in his ears.

Still shivering a little, Mark looked at the things that were close to him. The hedge, the grass, the trees were so strong and so full of their own secret growing that they felt to him like people, and people who were watching him scornfully at that. Looking nervously back towards the farm he was comforted to see six pairs of jeans still dangling slowly on the line, but he couldn't see any signs of their owners. He really was quite alone. No twins and no Tata, no Jamie or Hayhoe or Riding. It was a funny feeling that he'd never had before and he didn't think he liked it much. A strong feeling of self-pity began to come over him.

If ever he needed Midway this was the time! What was the good of having a friend if he didn't come when you wanted him? Longingly Mark tried to picture the tiger again in all his glory, as he had first seen him on the island, but each time that he tried he found that the most extraordinary and exasperating thing happened instead. All he could conjure up was a picture of himself.

The most mouldy picture it was, too; sulky, aggrieved and sorry for itself. 'Oh, get away!' cried Mark to this image furiously, and then suddenly, because it was so silly to be standing there and talking to an image of himself, his mood changed and he started to laugh. And just as suddenly, as the imaginary, bad-tempered Mark looked up, startled, and began to dissolve, something happened to the real one too and the most exciting and wonderful feeling came back into the air.

It was Midway! He was there and had been all the time, laughing with Mark at himself! He had just been teasing him! All right, so what? That was a game that two could play at and Mark would pretend that he didn't care either.

He started whistling. How he longed to be able to plunge his hands down into that thick, crisp fur again, but he wouldn't even think of it! He stuck his hands in his pockets and the feeling in the air grew stronger. Was that a green eye winking or the sun on a left-over dew drop? Was something moving ahead of him or was it just that the wind had shivered the grass into stripes? Only just managing to remember Eric Clay's earnest injunction to shut all gates behind him Mark rushed on, his spirits shooting up like a fountain. Of course he wasn't alone! Midway was there, very near, just the other side of a Cellophane-thin bit of air; at any moment, like a lion in a circus, he might crack it and come bounding through. Finding that he had gone farther than he thought Mark once again stopped and looked round.

One might be alone but there was certainly lots of room in the country, he thought approvingly, no notices about grass and seemingly no people to stop him going anywhere he wanted. He thought he would go and explore the forest, chase Midway in and out between the trees. To let off some energy Mark crossed the next field in a series of cartwheels and came up with a spinning head to see another padlocked gate in front of him. He vaulted it, clearing the top bar easily, but as he landed on the other side he stumbled on something unexpected and collapsed in a heap. He heard a squeal.

The tiger? His hopes leapt. But whatever it was hadn't felt very soft. As Mark came swiftly the right way up again he saw to his annoyance that there was no friendly animal in front of him, but a girl.

13

SLIGHTLY smaller than himself, the girl was sitting by a clump of moon daisies which she had been picking and she was staring at him with wide open eyes. Mark saw now that she had been hidden by the long grass round the gate-post and that it was her basket which had tripped him up.

He stared back at her for a minute, still giddy and annoyed with her for not being Midway; then, when the edge of the field had stopped swinging and got itself straight again he grinned. There didn't seem to be anything else to do.

'Sorry,' he said, picking up the basket, 'I didn't see you. Is it all right?'

The girl flickered down a glance at it and then nodded briefly before she resumed her penetrating stare. There was a silence, but not an unfriendly one.

'What's your name?' asked Mark.

'Tilney,' she said, still gazing.

'No, I meant your Christian name.'

'It is. Tilney.'

'Oh,' Mark looked back at her. He thought it was a funny name. For a funny person too. He examined the face behind the stare more closely. He seemed to have seen her before.

'Tilney Tompsett,' she said condescendingly, as though to go into such a long explanation were a great favour.

So that was it. Mark thought her dress was familiar and of course it was twin sister to the one he'd seen hanging on the line at the farm. He must have seen her face, or one very much like it, peering at him from among the cats and the sheepdogs last evening, when they had first arrived. He went on looking at it curiously.

He had never seen such an uncomplicated looking face, he

could have drawn it with a compass. It was smooth and round and brown as an egg-shell and the eyes were pale blue rounds too. Above them were little half-circles of eyebrow, as faint as squashed moths, and the mouth was another round pink blob down below. The girl's nose stuck out in a small point as if it were made of plasticine and someone had tweaked it out from her face and there was a sprinkling of small freckles spreading across it and on to her cheeks. In contrast to the roundness of her face, the arms and legs that stuck out from her short blue dress were thin and brown. A cross between a compass drawing and a pin man, thought Mark, but as Tilney's silent scrutiny of him continued he began to wonder if her character were as simple as the rest of her.

'You're Mark Munday,' she stated at last. 'I saw you last night. Coming across that field in cartwheels just now you looked like a daddy-long-legs,' and as she nodded her head in confirmation of what she had just said her moth-coloured hair shook out like a bell and then flopped closely back round her cheeks again.

In a swift, limp movement, as though she were made of rubber, she got up. She picked up the basket and laid the daisies across it so that their white faces were at one end and their furry stalks at the other.

'I'm going to see Watty,' she said, jerking her head towards the trees, 'In the wood. Coming?'

'I thought it was a forest,' said Mark crossly, to gain time. He wanted to do something quite different, not go and see this Watty, whatever he, she or it might be. He wanted to be alone, so that Midway could come, but how could he go off anywhere with this girl watching him? Particularly as he didn't know the way. He didn't know how to refuse.

'All right,' he said, but as he fell into step beside her his mind was busy making plans. He could give her the slip somewhere later on, nip off between the trees when he'd got his bearings a bit more. It was just his luck, another part of these stupid holidays, to have got a girl stuck on to him like a burr; you couldn't just tell girls to push off, like he could have done to Hayhoe or Riding or even a strange boy who turned up. Besides, the fact that this was all her territory, or her father's, made it more difficult still. They crossed the long-grassed daisy field and climbed another stile at the far side in silence, dropping on to a little rough track that wound in among the trees.

'Who's Watty?' he said at length.

Perhaps because she was shy, though she certainly didn't give that impression, perhaps just because she had this stupid girls' thing about being mysterious, like Evie sometimes had, Tilney obviously wasn't a person to waste words.

'Someone who lives here,' was all he got in answer. 'She always has,' and this seemed to Mark more and more peculiar as they wound deeper in among the thick tree trunks.

'She's nice,' Tilney added, for full measure, a turn or two later in the path, 'So's her cottage,' but it still seemed very odd to Mark that anyone should want to live in this wood. He opened his mouth to ask more about her but then shut it again. Question time seemed over for the moment and as Tilney pushed on through the tangling mass of twigs that now hung low over the path her face had shut up again like a daisy at night. Giving up and just wondering what strange thing was going to happen to him next Mark followed her blue skirt in and out among the tree trunks. Was this really his everyday self or had he somehow strayed back into one of his dreams again? He pinched himself and it hurt so he supposed that it must be actually happening.

After a while his curiosity got too much for him again. He looked back along the narrow little track they had taken.

'How does she get food and electricity and things?' he asked.

'There's a way in on the other side,' Tilney said briefly. 'She takes her pony trap.'

'Is there anyone else living in this wood?'

'Ssh! Wait a minute!' Tilney suddenly stopped dead, putting out a hand to stop Mark too, and then pointed down to the drift of last year's leaves at the side of the path. Something that looked like an old leaf but then took legs to itself and became a frog hopped quickly away into the undergrowth after giving them one suspicious look. She shook her head and moved on again.

'Not usually,' she said, 'but there was someone yesterday . . .' Her eyes widened again for a moment as though she was frightened, then she maddeningly changed the subject again.

'Come on, why are you going so slowly?' she said.

'Watty's lived alone for donkey's years, you know; I wouldn't like it. My mother says she'll have an accident there, all by herself, one of these days. I hope she won't.' She let go of a bramble that she had been holding out of her way and Mark, only just avoiding its whippy backlash, moved up close behind her. After a little while the path widened so that they were able to walk side by side.

'She's got pigs, of course,' said Tilney, still musing about the mysterious Watty's way of life, 'and there's the pony and the dogs and the other animals, so she isn't really alone I suppose ... Why are you here by yourself?' She suddenly changed the subject once again and turned round to give Mark another of her stares. 'I heard your father saying that you'd got brothers and sisters but that they aren't coming here. Have you been ill?'

'No!' said Mark indignantly, 'I'm never ill. I ...' He stood still again, and looked round at the wood. Why was he here? It was just exactly what he had been wondering himself. They had come out from the dark, tangly path, full of dead sticks and brambles, into a little clearing, and the sunlight which had only been able to flicker through the criss-cross leaves and branches now suddenly shone down bright and clear. And all at once Mark, whose confused thoughts had been pressing in on him like the thickly crowding trees, felt an overpowering urge to break out into some sort of clearing in his own mind. He felt that he must, he absolutely must tell someone about it all.

'I ...' he began again, but wherever could he begin? He wanted to tell about all the peculiar things that had suddenly started happening to him, about Dr Barth and the scene in his father's study, about the way they hadn't sent him to Wealdstowe but brought him down here. About having Eric Clay for a tutor and him pretending that he hadn't been out this morning when he quite obviously had. Then as he thought about it he found he wanted to tell much farther back than that; about Seb and Evie and her old Alexander, about Hayhoe and Riding and how stupid they could be; about Jamie and how he came to pick hops somewhere down near here. And about ... Mark shook his head, his thoughts had gone blurred and he couldn't quite remember but he knew there was something that he mustn't say. But the need to empty all the other things out of his mind and look at them, like a day's collection of jumble from his blazer pocket, grew stronger and stronger. The only person about to tell it to was Tilney and though she wasn't what he would have chosen she would have to do.

She was calmly chewing a grass stalk. Would she understand? Mark had got himself to such a state by now that he really didn't care if she didn't. All he wanted was to get it out of him and he suddenly realised the strange fact that it is much easier to tell things to a total stranger than to someone you know well.

'I...' he began, coming up beside her again on the path, 'I'm alone here because ... Well, it all started on Wednesday, you see...' and as though that were the first little stone of a landslide all the rest came falling out of him after it.

14

BY the time Mark had got it all out, not only what he had meant to say, but a mass of other odd things like sky-horses and stair monsters too, they seemed to have arrived. The path went on but Tilney stopped, stood still with her hand on a broken-down gate to one side of them and listened to his last few words.

She looked at him briefly but said nothing; then, as though she hadn't heard anything of the rest, she asked him what colour Evie's hair was. Mark stared at her. Girls! Oh, well, perhaps it had been a waste of time to tell her, but he felt much better for it all the same. As she drew in a quick breath and Mark wondered if she were going to make some comment at last, she suddenly surprised him by folding up quickly, as though she were playing Hide and Seek, and tugging him down after her so that they were hidden from the path behind a bush. Then, seconds after Tilney's sharp ears had picked up the sound, Mark heard someone coming towards them along the path.

Above the silencing finger on her mouth Tilney's eyes grew even rounder. She jerked her head sideways, towards where the path went on.

'That's the path that goes on through the wood, where I saw...' She only made the shape of the words, with hardly any sound, but Mark was able to get it. Once again he looked in surprise at her frightened face. Whatever was coming? What was it that she had seen? She made it sound like one of the landing monsters at least.

The crashing and stumbling came nearer and to Mark's imagination, infected now by Tilney's fear, the wood all round them seemed to freeze as still as they were and listen. Mark shrank closer into the shadow of the bush. The leaves in front of him were too thick to see through so he watched Tilney's face anxiously. As his heart thudded so hard that he felt the whole bush must be shaking, terrifying visions of a sort of woody Pog Borius sprang into his mind, striding towards them with root-like claws and a neck that rose up and waved above the trees.

Suddenly, as he watched, Mark saw Tilney's expression change again and her mouth drop open in surprise. As she craned her neck he slithered forward so that he could peer through the leaves too. Coming along the path towards them, whistling a little tune now, was no monster but the bouncy figure of Eric Clay.

'Mark! Mark! Are you there?' He was calling out from

time to time, but not in a very urgent way; it sounded more as if he just felt it was his duty and was quite relieved to get no answer. The tutor looked half-heartedly round about him for a minute, then, as there seemed to be no one about, he went bumbling happily on. His bulging shirt and the round calves of his legs under their wide shorts passed Mark and Tilney and then grew smaller and smaller in the distance till his figure melted into the green blur of the leaves and was gone.

'That's Eric Clay, my tutor!' whispered Mark, sitting back and giggling a little out of relief.

'Well!' said Tilney, and as she got up and shook some leaves off her dress she shook off her nervousness too and became her previous dead-pan self again. She opened the gate and went through it and as Mark went after her he had an odd flash of feeling that he had left something important behind somewhere, or failed to do something that he had meant to do. But it didn't last long for his curiosity to meet this strange person who lived in a wood wiped everything else from his mind.

Beyond the gate there was a feeble little track of bent grass which looked as though it were made only by the feet of one person and very seldom used. As Mark and Tilney went along it, treading firmly to give it more strength, the trail led them round the corner of some straggling elder bushes and out into a grassy space where Tilney stopped. There in front of them Mark saw a small, low cottage with tumble-down outbuildings ranging away behind.

The first thing that struck him was how quiet everything was, and then how strangely pale. As though centuries of rain and sun had alternately washed and bleached all the colour away from them, both the beams of the cottage and the stone between them were ashy grey. The only dark thing about the place was the ivy which stretched knotty arms in all directions as though it were trying to hold the walls together. It seemed extraordinary to Mark that there could be anyone living inside such an abandoned-looking place.

But as though it were a perfectly normal dwelling Tilney had turned her face towards the windows.

'Anyone there?' she shouted.

A bird flew out from a tree and Mark heard some water trickling somewhere but the front of the cottage still looked blank. Tilney moved up a bit closer and banged at the door.

'All right! All right!' A voice suddenly shouted from

inside, making Mark jump, 'I'm coming; I can hear you. I'm not deaf!' 'She is though,' said Tilney, as they waited, and to the accompaniment of a running mutter of words from inside Mark now heard the tapping of a stick on a stone floor as dot-and-carry footsteps came towards them and stopped on the other side of the front door.

The latch in front of them rattled, its ring handle turned, and the heavy, weather-whitened slab of wood moved inwards in front of them, disclosing the person who must be Watty. But instead of the wispy old fairy-tale crone that Mark had been expecting, he was surprised to see someone who looked as hard and brown as a nut, in spite of being so bent that she almost had to look up at them sideways.

'Well, Tilney Tompsett!' she snapped out briskly, 'And who's your friend? Introduce us!' and the hand that she held out to grasp Mark's and pull him in through the doorway was as tough and whippy as the twig of a tree. The only old-looking thing about Watty was her stick but even that, as she flourished it this way and that, first to point the way into the sitting-room, then to flick at a dog's bone on the passage floor, seemed to him more like a magician's wand than something which she needed for support.

'He's Mark,' said Tilney, and as they followed Watty in under the low beams of the dark and damp-smelling sitting-room she started ruffling one of the black and white dogs who had sidled in. They seemed to have these in all the houses round here, thought Mark.

'Mark Munday,' Tilney went on. 'His father's staying at our oast to write a book on something and Mark's . . .' but a new dog jumped up to claim her attention and she didn't say any more.

Although it was August, Watty had lowered herself on to the hearth and was now putting a match to the rubbish in the fire-place. She seemed to use it as a sort of indoor dustbin for it was full of old grocer's bags and butter papers, with sticks from a bird's nest, which had conveniently fallen down the chimney, on top. Flames shot up and shortly afterwards, as the room warmed up, curls of vapour steamed out of the old footstool and the rug in front of the fire-place. As Watty turned to look at him from where she was kneeling on this damp object Mark suddenly remembered all Tata's lectures about rheumatism and began to see how Watty and her furniture had got themselves so warped. He wondered if she knew or whether he ought to tell her about it.

Watty didn't seem to have heard what Tilney said and it gave Mark time to look at her curiously. The trees pressing up against the windows had given the room a green, underwater dimness, but by the light of the flames he could now see that the brown face was wrinkled with deep cracks, like a walnut. The iron-grey hair above it was cut short all round, like a monk's without a hole in the middle, and its length was so exactly even that Mark wondered if she did it round a pudding basin. If so it must be one which came just to the tops of her ears.

'Mark's on his own, eh?' she suddenly startled him by completing for Tilney. She evidently had heard after all. She switched round to look at him. 'Well, there's no need to feel sorry for yourself about *that*, young man. On the contrary.'

Mark jumped and then blushed. It was uncanny, just as if she had heard everything that he had said to Tilney as they came through the wood.

'I'm not sorry...' he began hotly, but as she turned away to poke the fire once more Watty winked at him and he simmered down. As he looked at her back now he saw that she was wearing a faded pair of corduroy trousers and that the shrunken jersey above them had faded to a streaked sort of pinky-purple. On this, as on his own bathing things at home, moths had evidently been feeding happily for it was full of unravelling holes. His approval of Watty grew and grew. He liked her brown face and her pudding basin hair and as a general rule, though it was different with his father because his goodliness was all a part of him, he thought it splendid to find grown-ups who didn't bother about their clothes or their appearance.

Still poking the fire, one hand on the poker and flapping at him good-humouredly with the other, 'No, maybe you're not,' she said, and she turned to grin at him once again, sending another network of walnut cracks across her face. 'But I'll be sure you think life ought to be a whole lot more simple than it is, don't you? And can't think why everyone can't be just the same as you are and you like everyone else? I know!' and it really was so exactly what Mark had been thinking that his jaw dropped and he gaped.

'Oh, it's easy to guess what people are thinking about,' Watty was feeling now for something on the shelf by the fire, 'when you don't see many. People's thoughts stick out all over 'em, like burrs. Except for this young Tilney here,' she looked at the round face on the other side of the fire for a moment and laughed, 'I've never known what she's thinking.'

She turned to look at Mark's face again and he wasn't quite sure whether he liked the idea of his thoughts being so obvious. It reminded him of something uncomfortable, but as the rubbish began to burn up and the comforting flames shot up in orange ribbons behind Watty he was only aware of being caught in the twinkling stare of Watty's eyes.

'It's no good trying to fit into something you weren't meant for,' she said eventually, when she had finished her examination of him, 'you've got to find your own way; just that and nobody else's. Don't you forget that,' and she gave him one final sharp look before she turned away.

Mark felt rather embarrassed and for some odd reason he started to feel in his pockets. This odd feeling that he'd forgotten something came back to him, though he couldn't for the life of him think why or what. As Watty sat back on her heels to open the tin she had found the two black and white dogs shifted a little as though to make room for another, the flames flickered at the sticks and threw their barred shadows outwards. Something pushed at Mark's foot and he patted the nearest dog and rubbed behind its ears.

'Have one,' said Watty, holding the open tin towards him and Tilney, and they nibbled at the ginger biscuits, gone beautifully soft and spongy, that they took from inside.

'Has Blanche farrowed yet?' asked Tilney, obviously bored with the conversation. 'Blanche is the sow,' she explained condescendingly to Mark, 'and she's very stupid when she's going to farrow, isn't she, Watty?'

Watty nodded her shaggy monk's head, bringing herself from the consideration of Mark to more practical things.

'Wild as anything this time,' she said. 'No, she hasn't had them yet. It's a worry; I'm afraid she'll barge about and tread on them when they're born. Would you like to see the animals?' She looked at Mark and as he nodded eagerly she hoisted herself on to her feet again.

The dogs rose too, two or three or however many there were of them, and Mark, still thinking about the odd things that Watty had said to him, felt once again this quick, strange little tug at his mind. He quickly pushed it aside.

Animals! They really were the best thing in life and all his niggling bothers were sent away to the unimportant place where they belonged. A very comforting feeling came over him as he heard Tilney explaining about Watty's pony and her cow and this pig, and her hens. This was the way to keep animals, he thought, just one or two for yourself, he had been looking forward to seeing the farm ones but there were always so many of them that you just saw them in a crowd, like people in streets; these would be private and separate, each one a person that you could really get to know. Like...

'There's Bella.' As Tilney's voice interrupted his thoughts a demure, mousy-faced little cow looked gently up over a gate and flicked an ear and her eyelashes at them. What was it he kept trying to remember? But before Mark had time to do more than pat Bella and sniff her warm hay smell, Watty had gone on crab-like in front of them. She motioned them over to the low wall of the pigsty and called out to whatever was grunting away inside.

'Come on out them! There's my beauty,' and as she grunted and cajoled too something like a vast whitey-grey battleship came heaving and edging out of the hut and into the open. A pink snout snuffled at their legs through the gate while Watty's stick lifted a flapping white ear to show a round, pink, humorous eye underneath.

'She's quiet enough now, but she doesn't like anyone going in with her...' and as Mark scratched at the white bristles with a bit of stick he picked up from the ground the great bulk of Blanche moved itself up and down, to and fro against it to get the best effect.

'Seems to like you,' said Watty, "Tisn't everyone she does. Found any eggs?' She looked over towards Tilney, who had been searching the dusty grass hummocks where the hens were scratching about.

'Three,' said Tilney, putting them into the box that Watty held out.

'Breakfast, dinner and tea,' said Watty, and she winked at Mark as she tucked the box under her arm.

'Tea!' Tilney looked round at the sun, which was about half-way down the trees, 'I'll have to go back, it'll be our supper time. Yours won't be till after,' she told Mark, 'Mum does ours first, so you can stay if you like.'

As Mark looked round he saw that Watty was busy pottering about among the hens; although he liked her he felt shy of her suddenly shot-out remarks and thought he had had his character read quite enough for one day.

'No, I'll come with you. To the end of the wood anyway,' and when they had said good-bye they turned out of the gate again and went down the track through the trees to join the main path through the wood.

'I don't think your Eric Clay's come back yet,' said Tilney, as she poked at the dust with her pig-scratching stick, looking for footprints.

'I wonder where he's been,' said Mark. 'Where does the path go, after the wood? And where did you see this ... this other person?' But talking to Tilney was like playing Snakes and Ladders and the look she gave him now sent him right back to square one again.

'It goes to Puckshorn, where the hop gardens are,' was all she said, refusing to say anything about the other.

Mark's eyes brightened. 'I wonder if that's where Jamie comes?' he said, but once again, as he said the name, this funny twinge, as of something he ought to remember, came back to him. It seemed now to be something to do with Jamie, something that had happened the last time they met, but he couldn't for the life of him think why.

'Could be,' said Tilney without interest, 'but there's lots of hop gardens round about here. Well, here we are. Here's where you jumped on me,' and with the first real sign of friendliness she had shown, Tilney flashed a quick half-moon little grin at Mark and then scurried off across the field like one of Watty's hens.

Feeling rather at a loose end now she was gone Mark stood fidgeting by the gate, with the wood behind him and the hay field in front. But he felt quite glad to be alone and he remembered the odd thing that Watty had said. She was right, it was lucky to be alone sometimes, he had never thought of it that way before. Because when you were on your own, without other people distracting you, you could remember things, like ... What was it that was tugging away at him now? Something to do with the long grass, something to do with the orange flames in Watty's cottage, the dogs, the animals...

Midway! Mark went flaming hot and then quite cold all over, he was so horrified. There was Midway, and he had completely forgotten him! Just because of stupid Tilney and the excitement of Watty and her animals he had let him go, his friend, the best thing in his life; in the whole world!

Oh, how could he! Would Midway ever forgive him and come back again? What did he care about Tilney or pigs or anyone! Oh, how right Watty was when she said that you had to be alone. It was the only time you could think. Other people pulled you this way and that way and that was what made his dreadful mind go grasshoppering off again! He must find Midway and explain to him that he hadn't meant it; he must, he must! He would go now and search the forest till he found him, look behind every bush, every tree.

Mark turned and raced through the tree trunks, calling and calling, turning and twisting, running this way and that.

15

THE low sun was slanting through the trees now and their trunks flickered past Mark like railings as he ran, making him more confused every moment. Where the shadows had gathered between them the orange rays pricked through in dusty stripes, but though Mark darted eagerly forward again and again, the patches of furry dusk turned out to be branches of criss-crossing pine needles, the white gleams he saw nothing but tufts of withered grass.

At last! A sudden flash of green winked out at him from a clump of brambles, but when he reached them it was only the sun shining through a leaf. As he struggled on the trails tore at his legs and hands and left thorns in him everywhere till when he finally stumbled over a root and sat staring at his legs stretched out in front of him they looked as though someone had been scribbling on them in red ink.

Mark pulled out some of the biggest thorns and looked despondently at the last one; it was just the same shape as a claw. He threw it away. It was no good. He could go on forever but he'd never find Midway; never find anything here but brambles and trees. Better go back. But which way? As he looked round to see, he suddenly realised that he was lost, good and proper; he'd come miles from the path and there wasn't even the smallest track within sight; only these rows and rows of non-stop trees.

'*... forests of the night ...*' Mark gave a disgusted snort. He'd had forests. It probably would be night before very long, too; he looked at the sun and saw that it only had another foot or two to go down between the trees. He supposed he ought to be able to tell the way back from where it was – old Eric Clay and his ramblers would – but he couldn't; he hadn't a clue as to whether the farm-house lay south, north, east or west. He tried to think where the sun had been when he and Tilney had started out that afternoon but it had seemed to be everywhere, just shining, in the same way that Midway had seemed to be everywhere, all round him, only the thickness of a leaf away.

Oh, whatever had he done wrong this time to lose him? Even to lose the memory of him too, all that time he had been with Tilney. That was dreadful. Mark had got clear of the brambles now but he plumped himself down again in some long soft grass to think. Just for a moment, just for a breather, before he tried to sort his way out of the wood again. Turning over so that he could rub his hot forehead against the tufty blades, his smarting legs stretched out in the cool grass behind, he tried to think.

But his mind seemed more than ever like a grasshopper now, skittering about in all sorts of silly directions and making him remember things like the pattern on one of Tata's aprons and the pigeons on his bedroom window-sill, or how he'd been balancing a knife at school lunch that day when it had all begun. But how had it begun? Mark wriggled with impatience, he was so angry with his jumping thoughts. If only he could keep them still like that knife so that they didn't wobble ... if only he could manage to keep just one thought in the same place ... the thought of Midway.

He lifted his face up from the grass and stared at a small beetle climbing a stalk in front of him. He flicked it off and then felt remorseful and absent-mindedly put it back again. The stalk bent and the beetle moved over into the middle to get balanced, and as it did so something suddenly occurred to Mark. Midway ... in the middle ... and the knife had been balanced in the middle too ...

Could that be something to do with it? Did he somehow have to get into the centre bit of his mind to find Midway? Was that the way he could come?

Mark jerked his head up, excited, and began to remember other things. Yes, that night too, the third time that Midway had come, when Mark had been looking at the stars, he had somehow got into this middle part of his head. It was a comfortable, easy part, the place you were in too, he realised, surprised when you were just happy, like the time in the car, or when you made yourself not worry about things but laugh at them, as he had done yesterday with Eric Clay.

Oh, it was all beginning to fit in! And when he wanted something, he began to realise too, just one thing, very hard, as he had wanted to keep his father's papers away from Dr Barth, then he seemed to get there as well. But never when his mind was all scattered about like paper blowing in the wind, when bits of it were wondering about Tilney and bits were on Watty and her old farrowing sow—yes, his excitement grew—that must be true, because even as he started to think about them now he could feel a sort of dipping in his mind, the knife-blade and handle going this way and that.

But ... He could do it by accident, but could he actually make it happen? Oh, Midway! Mark's longing to see him grew stronger and stronger. He shut his eyes and tried to think of this dinner-knife balancing, balancing. With the greatest difficulty he drove out the distracting thoughts that tried to come in, thoughts about Tilney and the tiresomeness of Eric Clay, worry about not being able to say clever things to his father, and tried only to let Midway stay. A tiny Midway, standing on the knife, ears flicking and eyes shining, balancing there like a clown in the circus...

Oh, bother! For the moment Mark thought of circuses a whole troupe of clowns burst in, jumping and turning somersaults, and the knife crashed. Furious with himself, Mark had to start all over again. You couldn't even want too fiercely, he found, because that sent the knife spinning too; you had to be calm. Nearly, nearly ... Still as a statue he lay in the long grass till the quivering blades quietened and grew motionless. And then suddenly, miracle of miracles, lifting first one paw and then the other, like an unbroken reflection in a calm river, the picture of Midway was there.

Mark scarcely dared to breathe for fear of losing him. If he had made a picture of Midway did it mean that he could actually be there outside too? Almost too frightened to risk the moment of looking he opened his eyes very slowly and then lifted his head, as carefully as if he were balancing a precious glass on it. He looked in front of him.

There was nothing there. Only the striped bit of grass and the stupid beetle, plodding along. Mark lifted one hand and then dropped it down again; there was no need to take it out on the wretched insect.

He dropped his head, banging it into the grass. Oh, what was the good of it; it didn't work! There was still nothing but the old bramble and bracken, the same stuffy tree trunks with flies buzzing between. To add to everything his scratched legs were smarting worse than ever and he moved them over to a new, cooler bit of grass. It was certainly comforting, damper than the old clump had been, and its blades tickled the sides of his legs as though they were licking them. Licking them stronger and stronger, but with a funny sort of rasp in the licking...

Quicker than he'd ever turned before Mark twisted over again and looked round. Then, as the flies' buzzing turned first into a familiar vibration and then into a song of triumph all round him, at long, long last he looked into the bramble green, sunset bright colour that now was really eyes and everything in the entire world seemed to be back in its right place again. He suddenly began to laugh out of pure happiness. It had worked!

But Mark was much too happy just to keep sitting and all his tiredness had fallen off him like an old skin. As he jumped to his feet Midway sprang up too, strong as steel and lithe as elastic, and leapt away through the trees. Once again the chase was on, but this time the hide-and-seek was a most gloriously real one; it was truly a striped face which peered round the tree trunks and really white fur which stretched itself out on the ground from moment to moment, pretending to be a clump of nodding grass bents. Something of Midway's strength seemed to get into Mark too as he raced on, clearing brambles and fallen tree trunks in the chase through the forest; jumping the little pools that flashed up, scooping down into the suddenly appearing streamlets for stones, catching the overhanging branches and swinging himself up into them then dropping down again into the springy bracken to laugh and run on.

He climbed one giant beech, chasing the tail that whisked its way always just out of reach in front of him, and went on up from one rung to another of the tall, ladder-like tree till he reached the branch just below the top. There, in a fork, Midway had decided to settle for a moment, washing his paws again as it seemed that he so frequently wanted to do. Mark climbed up beside him and found that there was just room for them both.

'Look,' said Midway, jerking his head downwards, with his eyes blinking over the white fur, like emeralds through cotton-wool. As Mark followed his gaze he realised that they could now see the whole wood spread out beneath them like a plan.

There was the track he and Tilney had come along and the fire-break paths branching off from it like arrow heads; he could see the gate and the roof of Watty's pale little cottage and where the path led on again. It must go out through the other side of the wood, he supposed, to the place where Tilney had met her bogey man.

How stupid she was with all her mysteries and not telling! But he did wonder what she had really seen. As he started to think about it he wondered if Blanche had farrowed yet and what the small piglets would look like and what fun it would be to live like Watty did, in the depths of a wood. As his thoughts wandered off again he suddenly felt a cold draught down one side of him, and a feeling as though a warm rug were being drawn away.

'Midway!' Mark looked back into the tree. The tiger was growing fainter, weaker, like a picture that was fading away. 'Oh, don't go! I don't care about pigs, or Watty, or anything but you!' Mark nearly fell out of the tree in his anxiety to hold on to his friend, thinking hard, thinking only of keeping him there, and to his great relief Midway started to come a little stronger. He wavered for a moment like a rainbow and then grew full and bright again. But his expression was still worried and ill at ease.

'Oh, Midway, stay!' Mark begged him, rubbing his finger along the wrinkled stripes of the forehead, blowing gently into the shining fur of the ears, 'I know I'm a grasshopper, everyone's always telling me that I am, but I am trying to learn thc rules about you, really and truly I am.'

The tiger's eyes softened; he relaxed a little and started licking again.

'But why do you have to go away?' asked Mark. 'That's what I don't understand. Why can't you be there always? Why do I sometimes have to forget you in between?'

The tiger's eyes, as he looked up at Mark in the sunset, seemed to shoot out a liquid beam of fire, but he didn't answer. Mark looked at him, puzzled. Was it he who had to work it out? Didn't Midway know? He tried something different.

'What's it like,' he asked curiously as he settled down again, 'this place where you wait ... till I call,' he added hesitantly, for he still couldn't get used to the startling idea that it was really he, dull Mark who had never been able to do anything, who could bring Midway or send him away. 'Is it really like "forests of the night"?'

'When you think of them it is,' said the tiger, growing vague again, 'and when you don't it isn't. When you think of stars and mountains and rivers there are those there too. When you don't think at all...'

'Oh!' Mark looked at the wonderful creature beside him, frightened to think that he was so much responsible for it. 'But I don't know about anything except ordinary things,' he said, 'I don't know how to begin!' His mind felt horribly empty inside.

'I think you can find out,' said the tiger reflectively, 'from where you are.'

'From where I am?' Mark repeated, astonished, 'but I'm only at home and at school and here...' and as something occurred to him all at once he suddenly stopped and stared. 'You mean like in the museum, and in those poems?' His mind went on down this unexpected track and he began to think of the other things which gave you ideas, 'Space stories, pictures like Mother paints ... even Tata's old fairy tales...?'

'That sort of thing,' mumbled Midway through a mouthful of fur. He was back at his washing again, seeming to have grown bored with all this talking.

'Goodness,' said Mark, dumbfounded. To think that anything so glorious as Midway could be connected with what Tata and Mr Bletchly told him was a most startlingly new idea.

They both lay silent in the tree for a while, feeling its slight sway in the breeze and considering, and after a bit Mark put one finger out and delicately stroked it down the ridge of Midway's curving spine. For a while he examined the depressingly empty hollows of his mind, then he gave a great sigh.

'Cheer up,' said the animal beside him, 'it isn't really all that hard. You only have to start, you know. The rest grows by itself.'

Mark stared at him.

The tiger nodded. 'Yes; it's like seed. You knew you wanted a friend, didn't you, but did you really think ... of ... me?'

As his companion seemed to swell and glow beside him, each gold hair shining in the dying sun; as the thought of the magnificent joy and comfort of him flowed suddenly round Mark like a wash of warm water, he dumbly shook his head.

'You see? It's all waiting in the air all round you, but you do have to begin. It's like turning on a tap ... If you think of mountains, for instance...'

'Oh, I can see them!' cried Mark sitting up excitedly as peaks that were jagged with purple shadow seemed to grow and tremble in the distance behind the branches of the tree, but then they suddenly vanished as Midway tensed, pushing Mark flat on the branch with one paw.

At first Mark couldn't see anything, but then, as he followed the gaze of the animal's narrowing pupils, he did. Coming along the path from what Mark now thought of as the bogey man's direction was Eric Clay, just as he and Tilney had seen him earlier except that he was going more slowly as if his toughly-shod feet were tired, and that some of the bounce had gone out of him.

As he passed beneath them Midway flicked a small twig down on to the path in front of him and another on to his shoulder. The tutor looked up, shying like a startled horse, and then, as though he expected something else to hit him, started to hurry on in a sort of jog-trot.

'That'll clear the path for us. What's he so nervy about? You'll have to go back now or they'll send out to look for you.' In one bound Midway was down on the ground and

Mark slithered somehow down behind him, hanging on to his tail and back and whatever he could grab. In happy silence they went padding along together till they came to the stile. The open field was in front of them and there was a man in it, calling the cows in. It was obvious that they had to part.

Reluctantly Mark put his foot on the cross-bar but then he turned round, jumped down and ran hurriedly back.

'I don't want to go!' he cried, 'I don't want houses or ordinary life! I only want to stay with you ... in the forest...'

'Without your father?' Was it a voice he heard inside him or only the wind blowing through the trees? 'But anyway you can't ... It doesn't work like that. I'll come again.' It must have been the very last gleam of sun that striped their trunks, for now as Mark crossed back into the field again, the whole edge of the wood was dark.

This was the cart-wheel field, and Mark, full of new energy, turned a few more across it.

'I will remember, I will learn...' he found himself saying as he came the right way up beside Eric, who had been some distance in front of him, crossing the field.

'Well, that's splendid Mark,' said his tutor heartily though still rather nervously, when he had recovered from the shock. 'And what are you going to learn?'

'Oh, about mountains and rivers. About ... lions and ... gazelles and' – he searched in his mind – 'about ... parakeets!' He shouted the last word out, laughing, turned a final cart-wheel because he really felt extremely strong, then, 'Where've you been?' he asked his tutor amiably, 'on a ramble?'

'I? Oh, no. Well, not exactly, that is. I've been along to the stream.'

'Where you went this morning?' Mark thought he'd try

and catch Eric out. He succeeded, for his tutor blushed, stammered and then gave a nervous laugh.

'Yes. Well, as a matter of fact it was – I shouldn't have fibbed, should I, but I didn't want you to start off by thinking me *too* hearty...' he gave a forced laugh, 'dreadful, wouldn't it be, to be with someone who goes out so bright and early every day!

'Well, the truth is, Mark,' he said confidentially, 'though I'm actually rather ashamed of seeming so tough and all that – what I really go down for is a dip.'

A river, thought Mark, and suddenly saw a vast one shining in the back of his mind, curving over into rapids, widening out into a sparkling sheet. He put some fishes in for Midway and saw them leaping, saw himself and the tiger swimming...

'Oh, yes,' he said, rather vaguely, much too enthralled with this wonderful new game to bother about his tutor's cranky ideas and Eric seemed surprised and rather offended that his announcement had fallen so flat.

16

SUPPER was ready when they got back to the oast-house and to Mark's great joy he saw that his father had come down from the study and was waiting to have it with them too. His work must have been going well because he looked easy and relaxed and as he smiled at them Mark realised that he had come back from his far-away concentration place and was ready to enjoy their company.

This mood of his father's was a wonderful one while it lasted, like the sun coming through clouds, and all the more precious because it wasn't always there. You got used to people whose attention was with you all the time, but when someone whose mind had been up in some sort of mountain-top place all day came down on to your level ground again, ready to hear all you had been doing and to join in and enjoy themselves too, Mark found it terribly exciting.

His father's holiday clothes, the nice old heathery smelling tweed jacket with leather bits on the elbows where they rubbed the desk, looked as friendly and comfortable as he did; he had a bright, budgerigar-blue tie instead of his sombre London one and his lion's hair was rumpled up into a country easiness and twiddled into spikes where he had pulled and twisted it as he thought. Mark adored and approved him all over again, and his own mood, full as he was of the secret satisfaction of Midway and all the things he had discovered, matched his father's. He grinned and Max Munday smiled back.

'Well!' He looked at his son's shining face, remembering how very different it had looked last week when there'd been all that bother at school and after that business with poor Barth. He and Mrs Munday had really begun to be worried about it and as he looked at Mark now he was very much relieved.

'Well!' he said again, and to Mark his voice sounded even rounder and fuller in the oast-house than it had in Sicily Place. 'This part of the country seems to suit you all right. No need to ask if you've had a good day!' but – blessed among grown-ups, thought Mark gratefully – his father didn't ask what he had been doing. He never did and, of course, just because of that you were always quite ready to tell.

'There's super, enormous trees in that forest! I climbed right to the top of one where it was all bendy in the wind and it was like being on a mast – you could see right over the wood and all the paths and people walking on them almost out to the far edge!' It was so easy to talk tonight that the words came gushing out like a spring of water and Mark hardly noticed Eric Clay give a start.

'Yes, I ... we ...' oh, goodness, he must be careful! 'I met Tilney, you see, the girl from this farm,' and he jerked his head towards the door Mrs Tompsett had used. 'We went to a very old cottage,' his voice went squeaky as he made a wide sweep of his hand in the effort to show just how far away in time the cottage had begun, '... and you'll never guess who was inside!'

To Mark's surprise Eric Clay, who had been trying to smooth himself down into the semblance of a correct tutor again, started even more violently and this time knocked the glass of sherry that Mr Munday had given him sideways. After some wild juggling he managed to right it before too much was spilt and then with an apologetic smile he made a clumsy to-do about mopping the table. He would have done it better, thought Mark, longing to get on with his story, if he hadn't kept looking anxiously up at him and his father; his eyeballs seeming rounder than ever.

'Yes!' Mark was enjoying having news to tell. 'It's an old woman living all alone!' and as he looked round to see the effect of this announcement he was surprised to see again what looked like a look of relief flicker across Clay's face. 'At least she isn't really old; she still wears trousers ... and there's moth holes all over her jersey ...' he giggled, delighted to remember this, 'and she's got a pony and a cow and hens and a pig ... I mean a sow ... that's going to farrow.' The words 'sow' and 'farrow' pleased him too, it made him feel knowledgeable about animals and farms and country life in general.

'Good.' Max Munday looked at his son with approval and wished that Ilona could see him now too. He was dirty, tousled and scratched and looked as though he had been first rolled in some bracken and then pushed through a hedge backwards, but in spite of his own effortlessly splendid appearance Mr Munday wasn't the sort of person to worry about anyone else's. The lively look of interest on his son's face seemed far more important to him that a clean surround to it. He had been worried lately that Mark was going to turn out a bit slow; it was something which had never happened to anyone in his family before and he didn't quite know how to deal with it. And all these fantasies about tigers, or lions, or whatever it was ... He looked once again at Mark, who was smiling to himself and stroking one of the dogs under the table – well thank goodness there wasn't any of that nonsense going on now!

'Where's Dr Barth spending his holiday, do you know?' He thought he had better try and put this young Clay at his ease, bring him into the conversation, but although Eric had seemed intelligent enough about Max Munday's work earlier on he didn't seem to have much to say for himself now. He only looked nervous and rattled the wretched sherry glass once again.

'Oh ... oh, I don't know at all, I'm afraid, I ... I'm not really in his confidence ...' and to Mr Munday's and Mark's relief he gave a great gulp and finished up most of his sherry. Winking at each other, they left him kindly to himself while he got over his spluttering.

'Is ... is your book going well?' Mark timidly asked his father. It was a long time since his shyness and self-consciousness had let him ask his father such a direct and important question, but Mr Munday nodded, surprised at Mark's interest and pleased to be asked.

'Yes – well, it's a thesis for a lecture, really, though I hope to write it up as a book afterwards. I'm nearly at the end of it though it's still going to be a race against time to get it finally tidied up. But ...' he looked quizzically at Mark, 'I thought Dr Barth told me you weren't interested in my work or anything like that?'

'I ... oh!' Mark went scarlet. So the beastly doctor had

told him. 'Yes I am!' he said fiercely. 'He doesn't know!' and then in a rush, before his courage failed him, 'Couldn't I help you tomorrow, Father? Like Seb does. Like ...' he looked at the tutor. He knew that Eric had been helping with the sorting out early that afternoon and he felt rather jealously that it ought to be kept in the family. 'Then Eric could go on a ramble,' he said.

Mr Munday laughed. 'Is that what you like doing?' he asked Eric, 'Well, I don't see why not. But couldn't you both ...' He looked up and saw Mark's expression and had a sudden inkling of what his son felt. He realised that he wanted to be trusted to do it on his own. 'All right; thanks Mark,' he said, 'that'll be splendid, I'll accept your offer and we'll give Eric the day off, eh? I expect he needs it after dinning sums into this head,' and he ruffled his son's already rumpled hair.

'But mind you,' he added seriously, 'it'll really have to be hard work. I've got to give the lecture early next month and time's getting very short. Is it on? Ready to work like a beaver?' He lifted an eyebrow in question but Mark nodded vigorously and felt pleasantly full of self-importance for the rest of the evening.

When he woke up next morning it was the first thing he thought of. The sun was pouring in through the window in his round wall and he squinted at it from his pillow and then rolled over on to his back. He was going to be just as good as Seb, if not better, he was determined of that. In a masterly way he would help his father to get his work finished so that he could give his lecture magnificently and win all the fame he deserved, and then sell the book and make all the money too.

'Oh, yes, Seb, sorry you weren't there,' he imagined his father saying, 'but of course it didn't matter at all, as it turned out because Mark helped me so much ...' Mark did a sort of lying down cart-wheel out of bed at the splendid thought and sat on its edge. Then he started thinking about all the other odd things that had happened to him yesterday.

There was Tilney, a funny sort of teasing person, like a puzzle that you shook and couldn't get right; there was Watty and her strange little cottage; her pigs and the cow ... Mark was up and across to the window as he thought of them and then, as he looked out of it, he started dressing.

A whole day in front of him without Eric. Goodness, there his tutor was, bright and early as always, just coming into the field out of the woods! But there had been something else wonderful about yesterday too ... As Mark tried to remember it an enormously pleasant smell puffed up the stairs and in under the crack of his door and the other thought vanished. There was Mrs Tompsett's glorious food and this morning, if he guessed right, sausages, toast, coffee ... in another word, breakfast! Suddenly realising how near to starving he had been Mark got his last shoe on, burst through the door and was down the stairs to see Mrs Tompsett coming in with the steaming tray.

Sausages smelt and tasted better in the country, there was no doubt about it; the sunlight made the butter more yellow and shone through the marmalade in the glass jar as though it were an orange lamp. It was funny, Mark thought lazily, how many of the good things in life were orange and tawny and toast coloured, and this funny old memory was stirring again when his father came in from upstairs and Eric Clay from outside.

Eric looked damp from brushing through the dew, or plunging in the stream, or whatever he had been doing, and his hair was slicked down like that of a kitten that has just been licked. He gave Mark and Mr Munday a smile that was all at once nervous and yet heartily beaming, as though to express his readiness to do bouncy things all the splendid day ahead of them, and as Mr Munday returned his greeting he gave him a considering look. The chap had been very good yesterday, took an intelligent interest and seemed to know what he was about ... there was such a lot to get sorted that he was tempted to change his mind. But then he glanced at Mark, whose face was already taking on an important expression at the thought of being his father's right-hand man.

'Ah, yes Clay, you're going to take the day off, aren't you? Making an excursion somewhere, isn't it? I know you're fond of those.' He gave Mark a slight wink.

Mark's cup was full. Not only was it holidays and the sun blinding in through the window, not only was he full of glorious sausage and with toast still to come. Not only was he going to help his father just as Seb or another grown-up might have done but to crown everything, with that one wink, his father had taken him on to his side, into a sort of amiable Munday conspiracy against the rest of the world. When breakfast was over he jumped up, shooting his chair back and over, and as he did so he stood by the window beaming at his father, feeling willingness and energy fizzling through him like lemonade. He really felt almost too well.

'Steady! You'll have to go a bit more softly upstairs among my papers! Right. Are we ready then? Have a good day,' and nodding to Eric, who didn't seem as happy as he ought to be at being given a day off, Mr Munday led the way upstairs.

Mark hadn't been in this room of his father's before, but he saw that it had already got itself very much into the pattern of the study at home. The large table in the centre held stacks of books, piles of loose sheets of typewritten paper and the actual little heap of papers that Max Munday was obviously working on at the moment, because there was his fountain pen and the carved lucky paper knife that he always used, weighting it down. All round, on the sideboard, on chairs, stools and anything that offered a surface, other piles of papers were flagged with markers, and held down with ash-trays, pen-knives, and even stones from the garden as Mr Munday had run out of everything else.

'Ia ... I B ... Insert here ... Page 6, Section 3 ... See Bonner, Vol. 13 ...' Mark squinted at his father's writing as Mr Munday started to explain what was wanted and what was to be put where. He was almost too impatient to listen because his fingers were so much itching to get on with the job and prove his worth.

'We ('he said "we",' thought Mark happily) have got to have them ready for Professor Worsley to check when he comes on Wednesday. That's my absolute dead-line if I'm to be ready in time; do you think you've got the idea?'

Mark had just started nodding when the telephone rang from downstairs.

'That'll be him now, ringing from Canterbury. Can you make a start then?' and Mark vigorously finished his nod as his father left the room. These telephone conversations to the professor were usually very long and Mark was fired with an ambition to startle and please his father by getting a really tremendous lot tidied up before his return. The moment the door closed he rushed to the table and seized hold of a paper to begin.

But it wasn't quite so easy as he thought. The trouble was partly that he felt so excessively well and partly that he wasn't used to dealing with anything so fluttery as sheets of paper. The sort of energy that was running through him now was so strong that it really needed an axe or a hammer at the end of it; he could have chopped wood, driven in nails, practically shoved mountains about, Mark felt, but these poor little sheets of paper only floated out of his fingers and crumpled themselves into balls when he pounced to retrieve them.

He tried to smooth one by putting it under a pile of books but that made the rest of the volumes topple over and their fall fanned up more sheets of paper. Oh, he must get it done, he really must! But by the time he had got that lot back where they started from he was so hot that he went over to the window to let in some air.

Like his own window it looked down on to the fields and the distant tree-tops he had been climbing yesterday. He stood there trying to calm himself down, so that his fingers would work properly, but he succeeded all too well and his mind wandered away. How wonderful it had been up there in the branches, how lovely when he had come back through the forest with ... yes, the memory suddenly burst back on him, with Midway padding beside him! That was the thing he had been trying to remember! How exciting to try and make places for Midway and fill them with rivers and caves; birds and other animals! His mind shot away into an imaginary country; something pushed up against him and Mark quickly turned and looked down.

There beside him, his front paws on the window-sill, was the splendid beast, urgently panting, his pink tongue hanging out as if he had come running from a long way off. He had come!

'Was it all right this time?' said Mark excitedly, ruffling the fur beside him. 'The forest and the river and the fishes and everything I put in?'

The tiger nodded briefly and started to say something, but in the joyful exuberance that was still bursting out of him, Mark scarcely paused to listen. 'Did you see the gazelles?' he said, 'and those green parrots and ...' but his spilling-out words stopped in utter surprise as the animal turned and bit him.

It was a soft bite, but it still hurt and Mark snatched his hand away. As he stood looking down, silent and indignant, he heard his father's voice on the telephone down below.

'Oh, my goodness!'

'Exactly. Come on!'

There was a ping as the receiver was put down and Mark

sprang to his feet. 'Midway!' he whispered in horror and together they gazed round the room. There seemed to be paper everywhere, for Mark had dislodged some of the weights as he jumped up and the sheets beneath them had floated off. They could hear Mr Munday talking to Mrs Tompsett now as she cleared the breakfast plates, but soon he must come up.

Mark got the first few sheets back, but though Midway did his best neither his teeth nor his paws were made for such purposes; the papers got crumpled, torn and scratched and Mark was desperately trying to smooth them out again, without any idea of sorting them now, when he heard the footsteps coming up the stairs.

'Midway...' He turned, but the tiger knew and didn't need any instructions; he was gone leaving only a brighter, warmer patch of sunlight for a moment where he had been.

'Mark!'

Mark looked at the floor. It was no good trying to say anything. He could have kicked, pinched, bitten himself. Just when he most wanted to be helpful, when it had really seemed that things had changed for him and were going all right, even with Midway trying to help him, it had happened again.

His father didn't say anything either, only his face expressed his feelings, which were all too painfully clear. He sighed. Wishing that Seb were here, Mark supposed miserably, then he looked quickly down at the main pile of papers on the desk.

'Where's that sheet that was on top?' Mr Munday asked quickly. 'You haven't ... Mark! That's the most important of the whole lot...' and Mark remembered how it was the first one he had picked up and how it was getting itself ironed out again, he hoped, under that book. He picked it out and handed it over to his father and as he nervously watched Mr Munday look at it he saw that the creases were still all too plainly there.

Max Munday drew the side of his hand across it in an attempt to straighten it out and as Mark looked down miserably he unseeingly took in the pattern of figures and symbols on it. Three threes and some x's and y's and some squiggles he'd never met in his lessons yet; he felt as though they would be written on his eyelids, like Calais on Queen Mary's heart, for evermore. His father sighed again.

'All right Mark,' he said with horrible patience, so that Mark almost wished he would shout and wave his arms about and be angry as Hayhoe said his father always was. 'You go out, old chap; this isn't really quite your thing. And if you should see Eric Clay again and he hasn't got too much involved in whatever he's doing ... it's hard luck to break in when I've just given him the day off but things are going to be rather desperate now ... tell him I would be very grateful if he could spare me some time after all. Cut along then.' He smiled, a very remote smile as though he didn't even see Mark and Mark crept out of the room.

Failure. He hadn't even the heart to summon Midway again to come and share it with him. Better for his friend to stay in the forests, he thought, as he went out of the oast-house dejectedly, and across the fields, taking the same path as yesterday. But instead of the green distances he could still only see sheets of paper, symbols and figures; small bits of his father's writing instead of daisies and grass.

17

BUT now it seemed as though there were times, the really bad ones like this, when Midway could come without being called. As Mark slowed down after his rush out into the fields, making his way towards the wood and determined to find Eric, he felt something push against his side. Midway turned green eyes up to Mark in sympathy and then padded on silently by his side.

'Oh, Midway!' Once again Mark ran his forefinger along the short, velvety fur on the animal's forehead but didn't say any more. As always, he found that he only had to think and Midway knew. It was perfect friendship. Oh, if only he could have perfect son-ship, father-ship, whatever the word for it was, too!

Not that his father's side of it wasn't perfect; he hotly

rejected any such thought; it was him. Oh, dear! It had seemed that things were going to be so different here. Away from the others and with the wonderful thought of Midway always near Mark had felt he could be the super, Seb-like person he had always wanted to be. But it hadn't worked, he wasn't, and now he had even lost the hope that he ever would be.

His head drooped and he went slower and slower, till a hard, impatient nudge at his side broke into his gloomy thoughts. For a moment Mark stared down. Midway prodded again, as though trying to make him do something, pushing him towards the wood. But what could he do? It was too late now. Still not speaking, Midway gave him a really hard bang.

As Mark stood rubbing his leg, light dawned. Of course! Typical! He had completely forgotten what he had set out for. He'd got to find Eric Clay swiftly, more swiftly than anyone had ever been found before, and send him back to help sort out the papers for his father, so that they could still be ready in time for the lectures.

'Come on!' As Mark's thoughts cleared, a sudden jet of energy spurted up in him and seemed to carry him along with it. He hardly knew whether he was jumping or flying or airborne on Midway's back as they cleared the field and the last little gate and found themselves running along the forest path. When they got to the look-out tree Mark stood panting for a moment to get his breath; his hand was on Midway's ruff and his eyes searched through the close-packed trunks of the trees.

'Shall we climb up again? Like we did yesterday?' he said, out loud this time, 'to see where he's gone?'

'If it's that tutor man you're looking for he went down that way – I saw him. Do you often talk to yourself?' It was Tilney, who had come silently from along Watty's fork and was staring at Mark as usual. Oh, bother her! At a time like this! It would have to be her. Mark looked quickly down but Midway had vanished.

'You don't mean to say he's gone down to the river to bathe again?' he said, when he'd swallowed a bit of his furious disappointment. 'He must be absolutely bonkers! He goes about three times a day.'

'River?' Tilney said scornfully. 'What on earth are you talking about? The river isn't that way, it's the other side of the farm,' she jerked her head over her shoulder, making her hair swing out. 'And it isn't a river anyway,' she went on, as it flopped back into place again, 'it's a stream.'

Mark let that pass. 'But I don't understand. There must be a stream, a bigger one than the ones we ... I ... saw yesterday. He'd said he'd been bathing there after we saw him coming back that way and that he'd been there earlier, in the morning...' Really Eric was the most extraordinary chap, perhaps he was off his head a bit, and Mark suddenly remembered how oddly he had behaved last evening, starting and nearly knocking over his drink when Mark had told his father about meeting someone in the wood; stammering and blushing and rattling everything about.

'But why ever should he bother to say he'd been bathing if he hadn't? He's always trying to make out that he's less hearty than he really is, not more; though goodness knows why I should care anyway!' His eyes questioned Tilney's, but they kept their usual indifferent blue calm.

'Oh ... people do,' she said vaguely. She herself obviously wasn't as much in the habit of giving a straight answer to a straight question as Mark was.

'But why did he go along that path then?' asked Mark again, frowning. 'If the bathing part of the stream isn't there it only leads to the village; I went towards it with M... with myself...' he corrected quickly, looking up at Tilney, 'but only as far as where it bends.'

'Went with yourself!' echoed Tilney. 'Who do you

usually go with? I suppose you mean that you went alone!' but behind her scornful expression her eyes had grown frightened again. 'I'll *never* go beyond that corner,' she said. 'It's where...' but she didn't even seem able to say it; she jerked a leaf off a bush and started tearing it furiously to bits.

Mark looked at her sympathetically, remembering the far-off days of Pog Borius and wondered who or what it really was that had frightened her so much.

'Well, Eric Clay did go that way just now, whatever you say.' She was beginning to be bored with all this talk. Then she brightened, as though at long last she had managed to see the makings of one of her favourite mysteries in it all. 'I'll tell you something else too. He had a bit of paper, a letter or something, with him; he was looking at it and reading bits out from it, as though he was trying to remember it, as he went along.'

Suddenly she giggled and gave Mark that funny, rare, little wrinkled cat's smile. 'I expect he's got a girl friend in the village, don't you? It's just the sort of soppy thing he would have!'

Mark stared. This was a totally new idea and needed some hard thinking for he still could only imagine Eric perpetually battling his rambling way through bogs and briars. But after a while he nodded; it did seem to make some sense. He'd forgotten all about that sort of thing, being away from home, but now he remembered about Evie and her Alexander and about one of the junior masters at school who'd suddenly gone very odd for the same reason. There was that one of Jamie's uncle's too, so Jamie had told him, who had fallen in love with a conductress and let all the boats bang together and tangle up regardless every time he rushed to see her bus go by. It did all add up, Eric's starts and sighs and silly goggling expression, his carefully-ironed pale blue shirts and the smell of his hair-cream.

'Yes. They do write letters,' he said, from the depth of personal experience. 'Lots of them. So you're quite right; that paper might be one.' In the music master days Evie had often tried to turn him into a postman and make him deliver them for her; at least with Alexander there hadn't been any of those.

'Well, of course they do,' Tilney nodded too. 'Like my Aunt Shirley,' then she giggled her funny little giggle again, 'What do you think that they say? Dearest ... Belovedest ... Soppiest ...' She shut her eyes as she tried to imagine, pointing her small nose skyward.

Looking at her, Mark began to giggle too. After the stress of the last hour it was a relief to think of something lighthearted and with his first hoot of laughter all his pressed-down spirits sprang up again like a released Jack-in-a-Box.

'Most smashingest ... plushiest ... lushiest ...' He struck an impassioned attitude as they tried out various versions and soon they were both giggling away together, so hard that they had to sit down on the grass. The sun was warm and the blades were soft and green all round them and like the yellow butterfly on the bramble bush in front, Mark's mind had flitted away from the thought of his father and Midway; from the urgency of finding Eric Clay and sending him back to help tidy the papers.

'Most gorgeous, romantic Alexander ... Did I tell you about Evie's one? Dead in B.C.!' and the idea seemed most exquisitely funny to them. 'What do you think Eric's one is called?'

'Oh! – Something like Ermyntrude or Eglantine.'

'Yes, sort of wishy-washy, as though all the colour had run out of it.'

'It's Evangeline,' said Tilney dreamily. 'I'm quite sure it is Mark!' She had been sitting on her haunches but she reared up suddenly like a caterpillar. 'Shall we track him through the wood to the village and find out who she is and what they really do say? I...' She suddenly remembered the corner again, 'I wouldn't mind going past there with you.' Mark nodded and Tilney's eyes sparkled. To both of them, as though Evangeline were a real, solid person, living in Pucksworth, the fantasy had suddenly become quite real.

'Yes; look, here's one of his footprints, after the wood we can follow those!' And as the butterfly flickered up and away ahead of them and Mark pushed on through the tangling trails of bramble behind Tilney, the thought of his mission fluttered completely out of his mind.

'What silly boots!' said Tilney, examining the footmarks, and as they both went on again, fitting their feet into his foot holes as they tried to imitate his stride, Mark thought that it was quite true. Even the soles of poor old Eric's shoes managed to be foolish, much too tough and arrowed with lines of great hob nails as though it were mountain crags they were bound for rather than mild Sussex lanes.

Really, it was bad luck on anyone to be so silly all over. Mark's geiger counter flickered for an odd moment of sympathy and as he tried to think up someone a little bit better than the washed-out Evangeline for his tutor he felt something that was stronger than the grass brush for a minute by his side.

Midway. Mark went cold all over. Oh, goodness, Midway and ... something else he'd meant to do ... But, against his will, his attention was snatched away again as he saw Tilney freeze where she stood, putting a finger to her lips.

'Wait a minute, Midway; I'll get away from her ...' There was a brief tug-of-war in Mark's mind and then, his curiosity winning, he moved up closer behind Tilney and let her pull him off the path and into the undergrowth to one side. As soon as she paused for a moment he looked anxiously round but his heart sank; Midway was gone. Oh, bother! He might have known that he should give his full attention, but...

'I heard something!' whispered Tilney. 'We're nearly at that – place —!' and her fright was so catching that Mark felt another shiver go through him. Through the bushes he could see their quite ordinary-looking path going on till it turned abruptly, the one or two large old beeches that bordered it, the ridges of grass down the middle and the soft earthy bits where the imprint of Eric's boots were marked, marching steadily on.

'Well, it looks perfectly ordinary!' Mark said to Tilney, feeling perhaps that he ought to do something to calm her down. 'There aren't really any monsters, you know; I found out that the stair ones weren't true, and even the one in the cellar when they sent me down once. Ugh...' he shuddered at the memory but then remembered that the object of this manœuvre was to try and cheer Tilney up.

'I just shouted,' he went on nonchalantly, 'and they went.'

'How could they go if there weren't any?' said Tilney. 'You're really saying they are true. Oh, listen!' She shrank against him and they both fell quiet.

At first, apart from the small twig noises that they couldn't help making, the wood seemed very still. It seemed partly to come from the hush which Mark always noticed at midday, but partly because from the unknown territory beyond the bend in the path, from among the thicker undergrowth and more darkly tangling branches, a sinister atmosphere seemed to be spreading out like a pool of ink. All the bold and comforting thoughts which he had been trying to pass on to Tilney vanished and he too held his breath.

For a moment the silence grew thicker and heavier as they waited then suddenly, just ahead of them on the path, they heard the noise of someone approaching.

Tilney jumped like a rabbit and they clutched at each other's hands; then, as someone came round the corner and they saw who it was they looked at each other, bursting with suppressed giggles of relief, and dropped down on to

the grass. Like a snake Tilney wriggled forward to get a better view, but Mark, trying to follow the trail of her blue dress, felt that his progress was more like that of a crocodile. She stopped and he slithered up beside her so that they lay side by side on their stomachs, peering through the leaves in front of them at the track that was now only a bush width away.

It was big enough for a cart here and was rutted with hard ridges and hollows. On the top of one of these was standing Eric. He had two or three sheets of paper in his hands and was looking at them intently, but as awkwardly as he always did everything, his fingers all thumbs. His expression, as he read a word or two and then gazed up at the trees as though trying to memorise them, was as soppy as anything they could have imagined in their wildest dreams. Tilney, imitating him silently, gave Mark a delighted nudge.

But a memory had been coming back to Mark's mind.

At the sight of the crumpled sheets of paper he had risen, first on his elbows and then so that he sat back on his heels. He looked round at Tilney swiftly, but didn't return her smile. Then suddenly, before she could stop him, he had jumped up and burst through the bush. At the sight of the sheets of paper everything had suddenly come back to him, reminding him of what he had set out for and why he had wanted to find Eric. Oh, bother Tilney and her stupid mysteries! Bother her for having made his mind grasshopper away at a time like this! How could he have ever let himself forget?

'Eric!' he shouted and the double effect of having something burst out like a bomb from the bushes on top of him and then of having his own name bellowed in his ear startled the poor tutor so much that he dropped all the sheets of paper so that they fell like leaves from an autumn tree. He turned half to pick them up and half to fend off whatever had sprung out at him, ending up in complete confusion as he recognised Mark.

'Mark!' he exclaimed as the pages fluttered up into the air and away. 'Whatever are you doing here, I thought you and your father...' but in his usual apologetic way he managed to look so thoroughly guilty himself, as though it was him and not Mark who had been so dreadful. 'I thought you were in the study.'

'I was,' said Mark flatly, 'but I couldn't ... I mean I didn't ... It all went wrong. Oh, look!' he said urgently, 'I'm terribly sorry about your day off and Evangeline and all that, but could you possibly give it up and go back to help Father? It's terribly important, there's only two more days left you see, and I wasn't any good at all. I only got everything all messed up.'

Mark's words were almost incomprehensible to Eric and seemed to blow about as much as the papers he was trying to catch, but the message seemed somehow to have got through.

'Evangeline?' asked Eric vaguely. ('But he didn't say there wasn't one!' said Tilney triumphantly, afterwards.) 'You want me to go back and help your father? Well, yes, of course, it's always a pleasure ... and an honour ...' For some unknown reason he blushed scarlet again and looked almost as though he were going to cry. 'Just a minute, I must ...' and he grabbed at the fallen pages of his love letter. Without waiting to smooth or count them, as though at all costs he didn't want them to be seen, he folded them roughly and stuffed them into his pocket, but as Tilney came out of the bushes now, making him jump again, he dropped one and it fluttered away.

Eric, staring at Mark again, hadn't noticed and Tilney, not wanting to draw his attention to it, tried to catch it without his seeing. A sudden puff of breeze wafted it up into the air behind Eric and as the other two set off down the path she hung behind and kept turning round, like Gretel, to see where it would come down to earth. Her eyes suddenly narrowed as she saw the paper, smaller and smaller now in the distance, come spiralling down like a sycamore seed and disappear round her dreaded corner.

'Mark! Please come and help! I've forgotten something!' Mark heard her squeak and looked briefly backwards, but he was now completely occupied in hurrying on, trying to make Eric go faster.

'Well, you get it,' he said. Tilney looked backwards and went pink with fright.

'No! It's all right.' Giving up the hope of getting the paper and running to put as great a distance between her and the corner, she hurried on to catch up with Mark. He was chivvying Eric like a sheep-dog now, to make up for lost time, pushing him first from one side and then from the other, hurrying the bewildered tutor back towards the oast-house. He made him go so fast that they were soon out of the wood and had crossed the fields and without giving Eric time to wash or tidy himself Mark almost pushed him up the stairs to the study, not stopping for a moment till he heard his father's relieved and welcoming voice.

At the sound of it, although his mission was done, Mark felt as though someone had thrown a bucket of cold water over him. If only he hadn't been such a fool, such a double, triple fool, that welcome would have been for him. He came disconsolately down the staircase and stared round the sitting-room. Then, for the second time that day and only because he felt that to be miserable outside was one degree better than to be miserable in, Mark set out again across the fields.

It was no good; it never would be any good. He'd meant to be so different here, alone with his father, but he was just exactly the same as he'd been in Sicily Place. He might just as well have never left there, he thought gloomily, and his mind wandered back to it, remembering odd things like Hayhoe coming to tea one day and throwing his weight about; Dr Barth giving them the wrong sort of, too-expensive Christmas presents; Evie reciting him some old poem about Alexander and hiccupping with sobs. Like going out of the door in the morning and hearing it bang behind him, the swish of the cars as they passed him and the traffic-lights at the end.

There was a cat attached to the next door basement who sometimes used to prance up the steps as he went past and follow briskly along after him, as though it intended to go the whole way of his walk to the path. Failing a dog, it was rather exciting to have a cat following you and Mark used to try to lure it along and encourage it with all the cat talk he knew.

But it always behaved in the same irritating way. After about three more basements had been passed it slowed down and at the fourth stopped altogether and started washing itself; he had never once managed to get it stepping behind him as he went to see Jamie and wandered round the park.

But on the way back, exactly where he had left it, it would pop out again, as purring and pleased with itself as though it had been with him all the time. And it was that cat that Tilney reminded Mark of now when she rose suddenly out of the grass to meet him, just where he had left her, at the edge of the wood.

He and Eric had shed her in their hurry to get home and Mark was in mixed feelings as to whether he wanted to join up with her again. On the one hand he was taking a sort of murky pleasure in his gloom and wanted to be alone with it, on the other there was no doubt that she did somehow manage to make life more exciting, even though she did do it in a strangely itchy way. From someone as permanently scornful as she was he found that it had become an odd sort of game with him to try and get an answer that wasn't disdainful, feeling he had scored some sort of bull's eye when he could get that odd smile to twitch up and wrinkle her face.

On the bad side again, as it came back into his thoughts, Mark realised suddenly that he didn't really much care for this business of reading Eric's letter. He knew that people like Eric and Evie got themselves into states over their Alexanders and Evangelines but they were their own silly states and Mark had a feeling that you shouldn't go poking into them. You never knew that you might not be in one yourself one day. But then he did wonder ... Oh, bother fors and againsts, there was nothing he could do about it anyway! Tilney was here and evidently intending to take up their walk again, just like that cat.

But unlike the cat, who was always too limp and lazy to

have any strong feelings, Tilney was more than scornful now; she was downright cross.

'Why on earth did you do that?' she demanded. 'Jumping out on him like a lunatic! Just when he was going to say something out loud! Something gorgeous too, I expect. If you hadn't, we could have gone on right into the village and found Evangeline.'

'Oh ... you mean Eric,' said Mark, to whom that moment by the path now seemed a very long time ago. 'Well, I had to get him back to Father; it was important. You made me forget.'

He was as accusing as she was, but Tilney was intent on her own purpose and so cross that she almost hissed. 'And I don't suppose you even noticed that he lost one sheet!'

'Then why didn't you get it?' asked Mark. 'If you're as keen as all that to read it? But I don't think we ought.'

'Because it blew right round into the dark part,' she said, and Mark, his interest caught in spite of himself, looked up to see her terrified expression. 'Oh, I'd never, never dare get it now!'

'Oh, for goodness' sake! Whatever's so odd about this person or thing that you saw round that corner?' asked Mark impatiently. 'Why does it frighten you so much? Has it got horns or long teeth or one of those wiggly dragon things down its back?' It was he who was scornful now. 'Why don't you tell me? It's stupid, all this pretending there's something so awful and then not saying anything at all. Not that I care two hoots about it, anyway.'

'I'll tell you ...' began Tilney, evidently beginning to feel she was losing Mark's interest and that she must play along with him to get it back. A good thought suddenly came to her and her eyes glinted. 'Yes. I'll tell you if you do one thing.'

'O.K. What?'

Tilney looked at him triumphantly.

'You've said you will now. You can't go back on it. I'll tell you about that horrible ... thing if you'll get me the sheet of that letter,' she said, 'the one that blew away.'

18

AFTER that, of course, Mark knew that he would have to get the stupid letter, but he put off the thought until he went out again, after lunch and an hour of belated coaching, and saw cat-Tilney waiting for him.

Surprising as ever, though, she didn't even mention it, and as Mark took this to imply that she never thought he'd dare get the paper so it wasn't worth bothering to talk about, it became more necessary than ever. But he wasn't going to do anything about it while she was there. They wandered off to Watty's, who told them Blanche was due to farrow any minute.

But after they had watched the sow for a bit nothing seemed to be happening so they spent a pleasant hour or so hanging about the farm and helping. Although Tilney was as scornful as ever because he knew so little about it all, she was different, Mark found, when she had something practical to do. With a screwed-up look of determination on her face she milked the cow, washed down the yard and after she had wandered off to pick some spinach for Watty's supper sat down to pull the stringy backbones out of the large, rubbery leaves.

Mark tagged along after her absent-mindedly, half-worrying about getting the letter that evening and half about something which had come into the back of his mind again and which he couldn't quite remember. And in spite of having got Eric Clay back to help his father he was still bothered that there might not be time to get it all done. He longed to rush back and start helping again too, but at the thought of his father's face that morning he kicked angrily at a stone, which went flying off to hit Tilney's milk pail.

Oh, dear, what had gone wrong with him again? He looked down at his hands and they didn't really seem all that clumsy. Like the time in his father's study at home the bother had made it go all confused in his mind and he had had an odd, ridiculous feeling that there had been someone else there with him too. But how could there have been? And it had all been so stupid because before those papers had started flying about and being so tiresome he remembered that he had felt absolutely wonderful, like a superman and able to do anything . . .

'Oh, stop mooning!' said Tilney, bustling impatiently, 'and give me that brush there!' and Mark, who wouldn't normally have dreamt of obeying such an order, came dreamily back from his elusive memories and handed it over. The afternoon went on and they had tea with Watty, who looked at Mark from time to time questioningly, and then after they had hung over Blanche's sty for a while longer and scratched her hopefully it was time for supper and to go home.

Mark hung back a bit as they neared the oast-house, wondering how his father would welcome him. But he needn't have worried, there was no one in the lower room and only his own supper on the table. Coming down briefly from the study with an empty tray, Eric put it on the table and fussed round busily for a moment before he started to bustle away again up the stairs. Everyone seemed to be bustling round him today, thought Mark, full of gloom, and it made him feel more useless than ever.

'We've had ours upstairs,' said Eric, his pale eyes glistening with a mixture of bother, excitement and importance. 'Your father's suddenly seen a completely new possibility . . . it will lead to a whole new development . . . he's got to get it down and in its place. It means a whole lot of alterations, of course

... I dare say we'll be here all night. You'll be able to look after yourself, won't you ...' and, cut off from all the excitement, Mark was left flatly alone.

'Just as if I wasn't here!' he thought, self-pityingly, miserable at being out of everything. 'I bet they'd never leave Seb like that!' But after he'd eaten his supper he began to feel better and a more dashing mood came on. All right, if nobody cared about him he would go out and get that paper; this was the time. It would be light until at least nine o'clock and he could easily be back by then. Not that anybody would notice if he wasn't, he thought, and his self-pity once again got the upper hand of him as he slipped out and went towards the wood.

As he saw its dark edge ahead of him he suddenly felt a shiver of apprehension, as though Tilney's fear had been hanging about there like a cloud of midges and now had come down to settle on him. But he quickly brushed them aside and the thought that he had taken on Tilney's challenge without a moment's hesitation made him feel bold and dashing again. He'd get that silly old sheet of letter, bring it back to her and hear whatever nonsense she had been thinking up for herself, then there'd be no more of this stupid mystery business which he was beginning to find such a bore. Then he could get back to his own problems again and fish out this something which was lurking at the back of his mind and which he knew was so terribly important.

Oh, bother Tilney! he thought again as he reached the gate; why was she always cropping up when he had other things to do? Being with her was like reading a comic, you knew it was stupid but you had to go on, just to find out what happened.

The sun was so low now that its dying fingers couldn't reach beyond the last field and the tree side of the gate was cool and quiet. As Mark climbed over and dropped down on to the path he shivered again, in spite of himself, because the wood seemed to have taken on a new character and become strange. Going into the band of grey dusk after the warmth of the slanting sunlight was like stepping into cold water and everything was so terribly still. At least, at first it seemed still, but when he stopped to listen he wished it really had been for he seemed to be overhearing small private noises everywhere, noises that belonged to the wood's evening inhabitants and were not for day-time humans to overhear. A queer feeling came over him that he wasn't welcome there and might be punished for it, the old feeling that he used to have with the landing monsters, up the dusky stairs at home.

Mark looked nervously upwards; the close-packed tree trunks above and all round him looked very dense, severe and tall. To have to go on between them, into the grey-green gloom ahead, up to the sinister place where the path turned, seemed a terrifying journey. For a moment he thought of turning back, then suddenly he ducked his chin down, pulled himself up straighter and stumped firmly forward, as though each step could squash a fear down like a spark. He was dashed if he'd go back! He'd show them! He was going on to get that sheet of letter and if something did happen, if one of the trees did get him ... pleasant thoughts of a martyr's death and of everyone being sorry flickered before him for a moment. Yes; he'd started and he wasn't going to stop in the mid ...

Mid ... Like a sudden clap of thunder full memory came back to him. Midway! That was what he had been trying to remember, of course it was! And then, as the realisation of what he had done flooded through him it was followed by the most terrible remorse.

Midway, his friend, and he'd abandoned him! Completely forgotten about the best thing in his life! All this time when he could have been finding out things for Midway to live among, when he could have been making more certain how he could reach him every time, he had just let himself mess about and forget. Oh, Midway! The longing for him came like a great wave, nearly knocking him over. How could he get him back again, would he ever forgive? Standing as still as he could in his agitation Mark tried to get back into that middle part of his mind again to think.

It did seem to help a little bit, because one or two ideas came clear. Mark knew he had to go on with what he was doing, that was the first thing; somehow he felt that Midway would want him to get that over and the Tilney business tied up. Then ... but he couldn't think too far ahead; only one thing at a time. All he had to do now was to go on into this miserable darkening wood and find out what Tilney was being so silly about. Now that he knew that and had made up his mind to do it surely Midway would come?

At the very moment that he was thinking it, and when the air did indeed seem to be thickening in the old exciting way, something burst out of a bush beside him, made a shrill whirr and then went clacking on its way. It was only a bird, but Mark's heart was beating like the tick of an alarm clock. 'Oh, come quickly!' he begged, wanting Midway before anything else awful came out of the bushes, but perversely the vibration in the air died down and nothing came.

What was wrong? Why didn't his friend come now that Mark had managed to drive all the distractions out of his mind? But had he? As the wood grew more shadowy and menacing every minute and Mark's jumping heart stoked itself up from an alarm clock to a piston thud he suddenly realised that his very fear was to blame. It was making a thick sort of barrier all round him and he must stop it, but how did you stop being afraid? He tried the balancing trick again but at every new sound and each lengthening shadow the knife blade jigged madly up and down.

Would it be better to back out of the wood again to find Midway? Mark turned and took a step back along the path but at that even the thought of Midway began to grow thin.

He quickly retraced his footsteps again; he had to go on. Although the thing he was going to do was so feeble, that didn't matter, he knew that Seb would have done it and even Evie, who would have braved witches or anything for the sake of the bandmaster or her Alexander; in his solid sort of way he was quite sure that Jamie would have gone on too. Well, so would he.

At the thought of Jamie a picture of his friend's face came into Mark's mind and he was dimly aware of the old park background of trees and lake blurring away behind him, though he couldn't quite remember what Jamie's story had been about.

'Cor, I was frightened ... !' He could hear Jamie's voice. 'When my Dad says, "You stand still, son, and take some deep breaths! No charge for them! It works y'know, you try it sometime ..."' Jamie's face and voice faded and Mark made himself stand under the frightening trees that stretched their wavering fingers towards him and draw in some of these long deep breaths.

It was difficult at first because they hurt and there didn't seem to be room for them but then, to his astonishment he found that Jamie was right. It was like giving his thumping heart a drink and it calmed down and stopped going off like a saluting gun. Without it bouncing about so much Mark found that he was once more able to think and when he did it had a most extraordinary effect. When he thought about the terrors of the wood, like Pog Borius and his peers on the Sicily Place stairs years ago, they went all wispy and shrivelled away. Thinking was rather like turning a hose on something, or when his father shot up the squirts of water on to the dusty windscreen of the car, and he was surprised at the power of it.

Because after all, said his mind, now almost laughing at him, what could there be in the wood? If these trees had been just ordinary ones in the full light, how could they be different now, just because the sun had gone down and they looked strange and grey? He jolly well knew that that the spaces between the trees were only filled with thorny brambles, so what was the point of thinking there were monsters there with leaf-like, waving claws? At the very word his mind flickered for a minute, like a nervous horse shying, but he held it down firmly. Monsters didn't exist.

And as for whatever lay beyond the part of the track they hadn't explored yet – well, it was obviously just some sort of game that Tilney was playing with herself. She probably didn't know about this thinking – he must tell her – and made mysteries out of everything; it was probably just some perfectly ordinary village person she'd met. Staring hard and fiercely, first at the dim tree trunks, then at the brambles and then along the path ahead of him, as though defying them to turn into anything else, Mark squared his shoulders and started out again.

And if Midway wouldn't come with him he'd jolly well go by himself. Of course there wasn't anyone coming along behind him; he wouldn't let himself imagine there was. There couldn't be any other sound but the crackle of his own footsteps ... not even ... not even a gnarly, scratchy sound, a soft muffled plodding that might be made by dragon's feet ...

'Well, I'll just jolly well look round to prove it,' Mark said to himself, after a few more hurried and not very deep breathings to try and keep his heart still, 'and if there is something I ... I'll throw something at it!' and knowing that if he ever wanted to see Midway again he'd got to go through with this, he turned.

A long tail swished in pleasure and two glowing green eyes looked at him.

There was a moment of silence as Mark gulped and looked back at Midway, quite unable to speak.

'I'm sorry,' said Midway, seeing Mark's look, 'but I just couldn't get here. You made a fence.'

Mark nodded and went on looking at the necklaces of black rings, taking in every shining hair and silken ripple as though he could hardly believe they were really there. He knew all too well what the tiger had meant. But why did it have to be that way? He wished he could understand these silly rules, whoever made them. When you were frightened was when you most needed a friend and what was the good of it if he couldn't come then? Or did it mean ... a little light began to dawn; did it mean that it was all right if you still stayed frightened but tried to do something about it? That made sense, perhaps, but why, oh, why did he have to lose Midway, and even the memory of him, as he'd done all this afternoon? So Midway couldn't come when he was angry, nor when he was frightened, nor when his mind went hopping off on to distractions ... Mark sighed, a long, long sigh.

'You know, you're jolly difficult,' he said.

But when the tiger lowered his head and then lifted it to look sadly up again, sending the striped wrinkles coursing along his neck; when he lifted one heavy paw gently and touched Mark's foot with it, Mark couldn't hold back any longer.

'Don't worry!' he cried, ruffling the fur. 'It's just as bad for you and it's my fault, I know! But I'll learn it all in time, and remember; I promise I will, I'll remember ...' At the very sound of words he did indeed remember what he had set out through the wood for and, as always, he found that Midway knew everything without being told. They both knew that the time for sentiments and explanations was over and that the time for action had come.

'The light's going fast,' said Mark, 'and I've got to get that bit of letter. Let's get it over with quickly and then we can enjoy ourselves!' And side by side, with Midway's fur brushing against Mark's thigh and Mark's hand in Midway's ruff again, they set off along the path. It had become a perfect adventure now, just exactly as it ought to be, and in the comfort of his friend's company Mark found that he didn't even want to talk.

They went on past the trunk of the look-out tree they had once climbed and then another one, almost as big, loomed up on the other side. Suddenly Mark felt his feet, which had been striding along at a good pace, began to go a little slower and he was cross with them. He knew perfectly well why, it was because ahead of them, barred by a dark screen of bushes and undergrowth, the track seemed to stop altogether as it turned sharply into the unknown territory and was lost to sight.

In spite of Midway Mark felt a little trickle of fear run over him like a fly and, holding firmly on to his ruff, he looked anxiously down at his friend. Surely he wasn't beginning to shrink again ... he wouldn't have to lose him now? Oh, he must do something quickly to show that he wasn't afraid! Immediately and horribly Mark knew exactly what.

'Look, this is the place,' he said as casually as he could manage. 'If it's still there the bit of paper floated away just round the corner. If you'll wait here I ... I'll go and see.' It did seem ridiculous, but Tilney's fear was still catching and it took quite an effort to let go of the fur. Mark was instantly rewarded for the tiger shot one green look of approval then seemed to grow and glow more beautiful than ever as he settled down to wash himself and wait, shining in the dusky light as though he were made of solid copper and gold.

Mark went quickly forward, telling himself that Tilney's ideas were all nonsense, his eyes scanning the ground. The paper might have blown on and got stuck in a root somewhere, but it couldn't be far and its whiteness would show up in this fading light.

Searching, and without looking up, Mark reached the turning and turned too, relieved to find that the path went on in just the same old bumpy, hummocky, tussocky way.

From the way Tilney had talked he had almost begun to imagine it as overgrown with man-eating plants and deadly nightshade, with bats flapping overhead and toads hopping on the path beneath, not with just ordinary things like this long, quite ordinary, home going worm that he could see. How stupid could you be, he was beginning to think perkily, bending down to pick up a pale leaf which it had just inched itself over and which might have been a bit of crumpled paper, how ... when suddenly he saw them.

There in the middle of the path ahead of him was a vast, hoof-like foot that was wrinkled and grey as an elephant's, its toenails digging down into the soft earth. Rooted with terror and not daring to lift his head, Mark slid his horrified eyes sideways. There was another foot! Behind them rose something that was massive and grey.

Oh, quick, he must call Midway! But the thought was just going out as a cry when he realised that was the one thing he couldn't do. If he didn't go through with this... oh, golly! As though he had cut an elastic that held his head down Mark let it come slowly and reluctantly upwards to look at the monster, thinking that his last hour must have come. Towering away above him, its grey trunk grooved and rugged and two of its front roots shaped like feet, with toenails and all, a vast, aged beech tree stretched away into the sky.

As Mark's mouth fell open he felt something arrive with a bound beside him, then the two of them started laughing as they stared up into the fan-like twisting of the giant boughs.

'They're mostly like that when you get to them,' said the tiger.

'What?' said Mark.

'Monsters,' said Midway, and he rubbed his gleaming shoulders against the scaly bark.

'We couldn't climb this one!' said Mark. 'Gosh, look at the width of it!' He moved nearer to the tree and stretched his arms out, even with fingertips straining he couldn't even reach round one side of one trunk.

'Look at these!' Midway was more interested in the insects but he looked across as Mark stuck a finger into a set of initials carved in the trunk. 'They must have been put here years and years ago,' for the letters had stretched out as the bark grew and now were wider than their height.

There were lots more of them all round the trunk. Full surnames, initialled hearts with arrows through them, stretched out dates of long ago and proper shaped ones of only last year, Mark explored them with his fingertips as Midway lay comfortably and watched him from the ground. 'P.B.!' he shouted, delighted, 'I expect it's the fossil of Pog Borius! Look at this lot – T.T., J.T., S.T., Z.T. – that looks like Tompsetts, but there ought to be two more if it's like the jeans on the washing line ... So Tilney can't always have been frightened of it,' and he stretched his hand farther round to see if he could feel any more.

He snatched it back quickly, as though he had been bitten. 'Look Midway, there's a hole here, where two of the split branches join. D'you think there's a snake or anything in it?' and Midway sauntered up and put a paw down the worm-eaten cavity. The tiger drew it out again with only a few shreds of old leaves and moss on his claws and shook his head, so then Mark put his hand and half his arm in too.

'Gosh!' he said, 'It would make a super sort of letter-box. Do you think that's where Eric and Evangeline ... Letter-box ... Letter! Oh, goodness, I'd quite forgotten why we came!'

'It's all right, it's there,' said Midway, nodding his head towards the grass verge, and Mark pounced on the bit of paper that now did gleam white in the dusk.

'Well, I've got it,' he said, 'and now she'll tell me about her stupid ogre; I thought it might be the tree she was frightened of but she must know that, so ...' he turned to

tell Midway more about it but the tiger, quicker to hear things than he was, was staring down the path beyond the tree, his ears pointing and the hairs rising along his spine.

First a wisp or two of smoke came eddying towards them on the evening breeze and then Mark heard the crunch of heavy feet as Midway, alert in every muscle, crouched low against the ground. As they heard the sound of a throat being cleared, in a way that was inexplicably but horribly unpleasant, the tiger and the boy wasted no further time but leapt away together, back along the way they had come.

19

THEY went so fast that Mark hardly knew whether he was on his own legs or lifted by the tiger to whom he was clinging, and as the distance between them and the monster beech tree lengthened he began to wonder whether he hadn't been rather foolish. Just because Tilney had met someone frightening there was no reason to suppose that everyone who came there was an ogre, quite ordinary people smoked and cleared their throats and were at liberty to walk in the wood. But it had been a horrible noise and then there was Midway and his hackles...

'Who was it?' he asked, but Midway didn't answer and it really didn't seem very important any more. Now he had got the paper and finished his errand, at long, long last he and Midway could really enjoy themselves. As they slowed down with his fingers still twined firmly in Midway's ruff, he looked round.

It was a queer time of day. The high part of the wood was bathed in a pale orange light from the sinking sun but down below the greyness of night was waiting to rush in like a pack of wolves. The sky above the branches of the trees was very clear and there was one early star. It was a time you never got in London, thought Mark, because the street lights were always on in advance and that was a pity because it was an exciting, sort of expectant, time when you seemed to be able to hear far-off things and think strange thoughts that you never thought before. As though each were answering to some sort of roll call before night came, every leaf and bramble flower, every pine needle and feathery head of grass stood out clearly and separately in its own right, their edges sharper, their colours faint but very clear.

It was wonderful to be out here with Midway now and Mark clutched tighter on to his fur.

'Don't let's go back yet! They'll never know I'm not there!'

'Where shall we go?'

Searching in his mind Mark remembered that dream he had once had about a horse with wings and about the sky shore and before he knew that he had translated his thought into a wish he and Midway were suddenly soaring through the sky and had landed there, running so that he could feel the sandy ridges under his feet and hear a great roaring whisper from the sea. Then he remembered that night at his bedroom window and they were rising through the pale sky towards the one star while myriads of others came pricking out all round them, spangling the sky like a net.

The little wind still rushed round Mark's head till he seemed to be drinking it in like water; a hand on Midway's neck was all that he needed to keep himself up.

'Where now?' sang out Midway. 'We've been to your dream place and the stars, where shall we go now? To the moon? To the Milky Way? To Sirius or Jupiter? You tell me and I'll go.'

Where to? Mark tried to think but he couldn't. With a strange sinking feeling, as though he were losing power, he realised that he didn't know anywhere. He knew the names that Midway was saying but nothing about them, he had never thought about anything but ordinary, everyday places and things. Even these started to blur in his mind.

'Take me ... take me to ...' he called out desperately, hoping that inspiration would come to him, but there only seemed to be a jangle of stars and the wind rushing through his ears once more, faster and faster as they went downwards; then Midway and he had landed on the path through the wood again. Mark came down as though from a parachute and rolled over and over on the leafy path.

He sat up and stared at his friend reproachfully.

'It's no good,' said Midway sadly, sitting on his haunches, his square feet planted. 'I wish it was. I can only go where you think of. It's you that's got to know.'

'But how can I?' said Mark crossly. 'How can I know if I've never been? And you say I can't go if I don't know; so that means never ... Oh, it's stupid!' he burst out angrily; it was just as teasing as Tilney was, as teasing as jam yesterday and jam tomorrow, but never today. Then he looked down in alarm. Was it that the dusk was growing thicker or was Midway really fading?

'I told you before, why won't you listen? You don't have to know everything ... only to start and to want to know! Then it can be added...' What was it that the tiger was saying and why did he sound so sad? Mark could hardly hear him now. 'But not if you get angry or think you can't do it ... that's the worst thing of all...' It was just the thread of a thought voice now and Midway was getting smaller and smaller, like a toy, like a china ornament on a mantelpiece...

'Oh, don't go? I will learn, I will try! I'll ask about the stars and moon ... I'll think all the time...' Remorsefully Mark remembered how old Bletchly had been talking about stars and things when he'd been busy catapulting Hayhoe ... 'I'll listen and learn where to take you – oh, no!' For like the vanishing square on a television screen Midway had now shrunk quite away and was gone. Mark was left alone in the wood and it was nearly dark but he was too sad and angry to be frightened any more. His mind was racing round.

Everything had seemed so gloriously easy when he first met Midway but to keep him was just as difficult as anything else. Even lessons seemed to be tied up with it; that was something which he never would have imagined. If only he had listened to Bletchly that time he and Midway might be on the moon now, he might be the first person to know about it; if only he'd known something, just anything, about the stars! And now, because he didn't, he was back here in the wood by himself. It was going to be quite dark, too, jolly soon, and he'd have to find his way out.

Mark saw that the trees had grown almost black all round him, then he saw a light flicker on between them; from Watty's cottage, he supposed. Suddenly he felt he wanted to have someone to talk to, someone sensible; he was tired of riddles and answers and trying to work out all these confusing things by himself. He turned off from the path towards it and soon the pale cottage walls were glimmering in front of him.

He didn't dare shout up, as Tilney had done, but knocked timidly on the door. Surprisingly quickly, as though she could hear quiet sounds more easily than loud ones, he heard Watty's dot-and-carry footsteps coming towards the door.

'Oh, it's you,' she said, apparently not surprised. 'You're out late, aren't you? Come in,' and for the second time he followed her down the passage and into the sitting-room. On a bed of warm ashes that shimmered from time to time as the draught caught them two sweet smelling bits of wood were smouldering and a steaming kettle was perched on top of these.

'Apple,' said Watty, seeing him sniff.

Their three chairs were still drawn round the fire and by the dim light of a lamp whose shade was brown with age Watty had been reading. The variegated mat of cats and dogs on the floor, too sleepy to get up, thumped lazy tails to welcome Mark.

'Tea?' asked Watty, prodding the logs under the kettle, 'coffee, cocoa, Bovril?'

'Coffee please,' said Mark. He had never been allowed to have it at home but he knew that it was what his father took when he wanted to keep awake.

Watty reached for another cup on the shelf beside her and for the tins which had coffee and sugar inside.

It was funny stuff, bitter even behind the sugar she piled into the cup for him, but it did seem to keep him awake, and awake was what he wanted to be just now. They drank on in silence for a while.

'What's up?' asked Watty. 'Though you don't have to tell me if you don't want.'

Mark shot her an appreciative glance but she wasn't looking at him; her berry eyes were on the shimmering ashes of the fire. He looked at them too and as the ashes glowed red and faded into grey again he suddenly felt that it would be much easier to talk this way, without actually looking at her. He stared at the embers and tried to begin.

'It's about someone I've got ... about a tiger ...'

'A tiger?' she repeated, quite unsurprised, then 'Oh, my goodness! Mark! Did you hear something? What was that?' Watty had risen half out of her chair as a long strange cry, like that of some undersea monster had suddenly bellowed round the house.

'Blanche!' cried Watty, 'she must be farrowing. No, don't come out with me, you'll upset her. Wait here a minute,' and completely practical now and with surprising speed she had grabbed her stick and dot-and-carried away out of the door.

Mark, who had shot to his feet, sat down again. He was glad, in a way, that it had happened like this because as he calmed down he knew that it wasn't really right to tell about Midway to anyone, however easy they were to talk to; it was just something you couldn't do. Perhaps it was Midway himself who had stopped him going on. Oh, but how he wished he could get him back again! Mark tried, but he must be too tired or sleepy, or too much wondering about Blanche and after a few moments of idleness he picked up

Watty's book from the floor for want of something better to do.

Poetry! Was that what she read, all alone here in the evenings? He had thought it would be a manual of pig keeping or something like that. Was that how Watty managed to live alone and seem wise about everything? He looked at a page. There was something about a tree

'That burns in glorious Araby . . .'

His eyes slid on,

'Half buried to her flaming breast
In this bright tree she makes her nest . . .'

A bird it seemed to be about, something called a phoenix. Midway's sort of bird, Mark thought and he liked it. He turned to another.

'When I was but thirteen or so
I went into a golden land,
Chimborazo, Kotopaxi . . .'

Those were mountains, he knew that. This was the sort of thing he wanted to find out about! But before he could dive properly into the thought of their golden summits the door had swung open again and Watty was back. She held a basket in both hands, so that, without being able to use her stick she was limping badly, and she thankfully pushed the basket into Mark's arms as he got up to help her.

'Mark,' she said. 'You'll have to look after them . . .' She gave him a hurried, searching look and then peered down at the basket, which to Mark's startled eyes seemed to be moving.

'Blanche's; she's gone berserk,' she said briefly. 'Trying to tread on them all. There were only three so I've brought them in here. I'll have to go for the vet, or she'll damage herself. Can you watch them? Look – put the basket by the fire and I'll be back in a minute,' and she hurried out of the room.

Mark gingerly lifted the cloth and saw three whity-pink mounds inside. Before he had time to think Watty was back. She had a tin of some sort of dried milk in one hand and a measuring jug, spoon and rubber teated bottle on a tray.

'You may have to feed them,' she said, before he could protest. 'Spoonful to an ounce of water – lukewarm,' and she had grabbed her coat and was at the door before he could say anything in reply.

'Back in an hour,' she said, 'if I'm lucky – got to get the trap out. Keep them warm; warmth's life and death when they're so small,' and then she was gone and he heard the door banging behind her.

'I'll tell your father you're here.' She had poked her head in at the window and then Mark was really alone. In a strange cottage in the middle of a wood with three new-born small animals in a basket in front of him. Oh, gosh! he thought. He had never been so nervous in his life. Whatever did he do?

He gingerly touched the cloth that covered the heaving mound of small backs. It gave him a strange, frightening feeling that his life had suddenly moved a step further on than he was ready for. Life and death, Watty had said, and it was in his hands, but it gave him a pleased and important feeling as well as a frightened one. He was sure nothing as serious as this had ever happened to Seb or Evie, or to Riding or Hayhoe either. But it wasn't any good just feeling important, he had to do something. These small things that he was so nervous of had to be kept warm. There were only two small logs left in the wood basket and he hurriedly put them on the ashes. Then he lifted the cloth again.

The three pink backs all looked like part of one wriggling sea monster; Mark put out a finger to touch a bit of it, to see if it was warm. It was so silky, astonishing him as he remembered Blanche's rugged hide, and he ran his finger a little farther down the length of the tiny spine. A straight little tail suddenly broke away from the mass and twitched itself, then, at the other end, a head came up and there was a perfect miniature pig foolishly looking at him. Mark gave a funny little noise himself and curved both hands to pick it up and look at it. This was something to hold on to, easier

than those flimsy papers of his father's had been. Tiny legs with perfect small hooves hung down for a minute, then it started to kick.

'Hey!' Mark was astonished at its tiny strength and protested as one of the miniscule trotters scrabbled against him, and then somehow, as he spoke to the animal, a strange thing happened and they both became aware of each other. The baby animal butted its head against him and Mark felt the warmth of its small, sparsely-haired body. He saw one of its eyes now, such a very short time opened and such a very new blue.

It still felt warm all right and he had an instinct to go on holding it against him to keep it so. But the other two, now that this one bit of warmth had been taken away from between them, were protesting, with faint little squeals. Quickly Mark put his first friend down and it wove itself back among them again.

One of the three was much smaller than the others, Mark saw and to his alarm he saw that it was shivering; the last one was larger and far more energetic than either of the other two. Its voice was growing louder every minute and he felt he could almost see it growing as he watched.

He didn't think that the smallest one could be all right, they were such very long, regular shivers. 'Oh, Small,' said Mark anxiously and cupped his hands round that one to pick it up too. It was much colder than the first one had been and he put it under his coat and then into what seemed the warmest part of himself, under his armpit. Its racking shivers quietened a little, but now, lacking its hot-water bottle presence between them, the other two began to get unhappy. The large one, the squealer, was yelling its head off and even the middle one, a funny-looking little pig with a sort of cows'-lick of hair, had started to shake too.

Oh, dear, what could he do, thought Mark, distracted; he couldn't pick them all up! He put Small back again and pushed the box nearer to the dying embers. The logs had burnt themselves out quickly without seeming to add anything to the heat. Draughts, which Mark never noticed in ordinary life, seemed to be trickling in like cold streams of water so he dragged down the cushions from the chairs and propped them round the box. Still the cold air came in over the top.

Perhaps he ought to feed them? That would warm them

up, but he knew that the ash wouldn't even be warm enough to heat the water. He must find something to burn! But though Mark looked urgently round for a hidden bit of coal, wood, anything, there was nothing there. Wondering wildly if he could burn some of the books he bent over the box, as though trying somehow to put some of his own life and warmth into it. He put his hands on the two smallest pigs but he was so anxious by now that his hands were almost as cold and trembling as the pigs themselves. To his dismay he realised that even Squealer's protests were beginning to get weaker.

Mark leant closer and closer as he tried to breathe some warm breath among them, but his breath seemed to have got cold too and only ruffled the little hairs on their shivering backs. He took his coat off and put it over them, trying to keep their heads out so they wouldn't suffocate, but though two of the heads still seemed all right when he moved them Small's seemed strangely listless. So listless that even town-bred Mark, who had never had anything to do with the death and birth of animals, knew that it was in a very bad way.

Oh, what could he do! The ashes weren't even live enough to warm his cheeks now, though he was bent so low that he was practically touching the fire. There was scarcely any more sound from the small creatures than from the ashes. As Mark looked up and round the room in the silence he had a most strange feeling that there were two other presences there, towering up out of the shadows and almost as strong as people; both of them waiting, like players in a game.

Oh, no! Mark looked down at the tiny, shivering pig and knew which of the powers wanted it. Oh, no! he cried inside. It mustn't die! It wasn't because of Watty, much though he liked her, or even because he didn't want to be a failure again, it wasn't because of anything at all except that he just knew the piglet mustn't go. It was so new, it had only had an hour's life; it mustn't give in.

Oh, no, he begged it for the third time, putting his head right down and his cheek against its cold little flank. 'You mustn't, Small; you mustn't!' and somehow he felt that just with his will he could help to keep it there. As the small side grew even colder he pushed this will out of him like a sort of electricity and went on pushing and pushing it, forgetting himself, Watty, the cottage, his father and everything; only determined somehow to keep alight this small flicker of life.

And then suddenly, just when he didn't think he could go on any longer, there was a new warmth all round them and he heard the sound of a rough tongue licking the shivering skin. The small eyes opened for a moment as though in pleased astonishment and then shut again, but lightly and not in that desperate, screwed-up way. The two other little pigs drew up against the warm fur that now surrounded them and almost lost themselves in it. Their shivers slowly died down and as the ashes flared up mysteriously and the shadows retreated Mark felt the frightening presences had stolen away from the room too.

'Better get some wood,' said Midway comfortably, and as Mark looked at him he felt such a rush of thankfulness that it seemed to shoot him to his feet and out of the room as though he were jet-propelled. As he came back with the new logs he had found, the hard, brittle dry sort which burn up in an instant, he got the fire blazing again and heated the water in the saucepan. Encouraged by Midway, he somehow managed to deal with the unaccustomed job of mixing up the food.

'Here come on ... tch, tch ... you, Squealer ... oh, come on Small!'

'They're not chickens,' said Midway sleepily. 'You'll have to pick each one up separately ...' but even before he had finished speaking Small had smelt the milk food and feebly rushed for the rubber teat, which he sucked in a frenzy. As Mark saw the level shrink down and the force of the sucking jaws he looked across the hearth in astonished delight. Midway, a length of warm orange fur stretched out on the hearth-stones, was tidying himself up now, occasionally putting out an absent-minded paw to restrain one of the wandering small piglets.

'Not my usual job,' he was starting to say in mild surprise when there were other voices outside.

'I don't suppose...' Mark heard the front-door latch click and Watty's voice saying this to someone, as they came down the passage towards the sitting-room. 'I don't suppose that any of them can be alive still, but there was nothing else I could do. I had to leave them.'

Watty came in, with Mr Castle, the vet, behind her, just in time to see Cowslick, the middle piglet, swig the last white inch from the bottle. The other two, with happy, balloon-like stomachs, were asleep on Mark's coat, on the hearth outside the box.

'All alive?' asked Watty, astonished. 'And out of the box already?' But as she looked at Mark he was watching the shadowy shape of something that seemed to be slipping from the room. 'Good heavens, we'll have to make a vet of you!' she said.

'That's what I've decided to be,' Mark said, surprised to find it was perfectly true, but the last words started slurring off for he suddenly felt as sleepy as the pigs were.

The rest of the evening, or night as it turned out to be when Mark went out into it with Mr Castle, seemed to be covered in thick mist. Through it Mark was aware of the dark trees all round and their rustling, remembered being pushed into the vet's car and jolting in it over the ruts of the lane. He remembered a smoother bit of road, when it was his own head that kept jerking down in sleep and then waking itself up again with the shock, and coming round to the farm and oast-house by the front entrance.

He came to for a brief moment as they got out, full of the importance of having three small pigs to his credit and the joy of knowing what he wanted to be at long last. He was bursting to tell his father.

'Father, I...' he started, but it all fell rather flat. Max Munday, who had found that this morning's idea was like a fast running gun-powder trail that seemed to be setting off one exciting new conclusion after another, had to get them all into order again and was in his farthest away and most distracted mood. It might have been tea time or Easter, or Mark just have come in from an ordinary walk for all the surprise that his father showed.

Splendid looking as ever, even in this state of disarray, he looked vaguely up from the sea of papers at Mark and Mr Castle and scarcely seemed to know which was which. Mark swallowed. Just when he really did have something good to tell him! But this was much more important, he told himself loyally; of course it was! But there was something about Mark's look of disappointment which made Mr Munday look at his son more closely.

'Ah, yes, Mark,' he said. 'I remember someone did telephone to tell me you were getting back late; I'd quite forgotten.

'Clay's gone to bed, you know,' he went on. 'Things have got to the stage when I can only sort them myself. I've got to get over to Canterbury tomorrow and Thursday's zero hour. There's something else happening tomorrow, what was it now? Oh, yes – a telegram came while you were out. Seb and Evie will be here in the evening, on their way back from France, just for the night. You'll like that, won't you?'

His papers were calling him back and the beam of his attention was wavering off Mark again, and Mark wandered sleepily away upstairs. He felt a little bit dashed. He'd hoped, now that they had got into touch again, that he could have told his father all about everything tomorrow, about the pigs and him being a vet and even about those two strange presences perhaps but it wasn't any good now; by the time his father was relaxed again and ready to listen Seb and Evie would be there to hold the floor. And they'd have things to tell about France, of course, goodness only knows what.

Half asleep already Mark had dragged himself up to the top step by now and had his hand on his bedroom door. But in a strange way he found it didn't matter so much, even if he couldn't tell anyone, there was so much satisfaction inside himself. He could still go and see his piglets by himself, couldn't he? He could watch them and study them and see them grow. In a way, because he had saved them, they seemed to belong to him, but as he pushed the door open and shuffled in he remembered that it wasn't really he who had kept them alive, it was...

He just managed to get his clothes off and fall into the bed, under the blankets, and his hand, as he stretched it out to switch the light off, brushed against fur.

It had been Midway. With a sigh of utter, deep satisfaction he fell into a dream of trees, stars and magic forests; of winged beasts that cleared their throats and Evangeline carving hearts on a beech tree, and the piece of paper in his pocket, that he and Midway had been to so much trouble to get hold of, lay crumpled unnoticed in his shorts on the floor.

20

Mr Munday must have left instructions that Mark wasn't to be disturbed because when he did at last wake and see the sunshine pouring in he knew quite certainly that it was rich stuff of about ten o'clock, as different from what came in at seven or eight as golden syrup was from barley water. After blinking lazily at it for a while he rolled over on to his back and as the onion skin layers of sleep started to peel away from his mind he gradually remembered what had happened yesterday.

The last, and rather tiresome, thing came up first. His father had said that Seb and Evie were coming here. As Mark looked at a wavering splodge of sunlight on the ceiling his spirits sank. Not that he didn't want to see them, he did; it was just ... He rolled his head on the pillow to clear his thoughts. Just that he wished they'd given him a little longer to firm up in his new, last night's self.

He'd meant to be so different here, and at long last it did seem that he really might be and that it would last till he got back to London. But it was too soon for him to see his brother and sister yet; he knew that the moment he did he would sink back again into the old Mark who always did everything wrong and had his mouth full when anyone asked him a question. He rolled his head more violently as his visions of being his father's right-hand man, his mother's artistic adviser, even of nonchalantly confronting Dr Barth and telling him where he got off, without minding his dangling finger any more, faded away. Visions of taking in everything Mr Bletchly told him, so that he could suck in lessons like a sort of magnet; of holding forth knowledgeably to Hayhoe and Riding, and even of Seb wandering into his room of an evening to hear about his plans for becoming a vet, went too.

A vet! Mark suddenly slipped himself upright, the sheets shooting off on to the floor as another skin peeled from his brain. His pigs! How were they? In this morning's sunlight he could hardly believe that it had all happened or in the crumbling ash and lamp-lit silence of Watty's room with those funny little squeakings going on ... with the wavering shadows that had towered up like living things behind him and that something else, something warm and comforting ... Mark shook his head. Oh, there were so many things crowding into his brain to remember! And why had he been in Watty's cottage at that time anyway?

Goodness! Now he remembered the very first thing about yesterday and why he had been there at all; it was that silly old bit of letter that Tilney had egged him on to retrieve for her. She'd said that if he got it she would tell him about the stupid bogey man. As if he cared! Of course it was all nonsense, he told himself, but all the same he couldn't help shivering as he remembered the enormous, elephant-smooth branches of the tree twining up and the horrible way that the man had cleared his throat. Oh, really! He was getting as silly as Tilney and anyway there had been something good about yesterday evening too, something lovely, though he couldn't seem to remember what.

But his thoughts rushed back to their best place again. This new idea of being a vet, this glorious certainty of knowing what he wanted to be at all, was so very much more important than any of Tilney's nonsense. Besides, he thought, remembering the first bit of news, if it was anything to do with love letters, now that Evie was coming he reckoned that Tilney would do much better to go to her. Evie was the expert and in France she had probably grown some wild new passion that would put everyone else's in the shade.

No, his animals were what he wanted, not to be playing babies' games about Eric and Evangeline. He shot out of bed and started dressing. The moment breakfast was over he'd go down to see how Cowslick and Squealer and Small were doing. That is if anyone had left him any breakfast at this late hour.

They had. The eggs were still warm under their cover and although the toast had gone limp and squeaky it still made a raft for butter and marmalade, which was what he reckoned toast was for. Mr Munday had evidently left for last night's overflow of papers had shrunk back out of the sitting-room again and when Mark looked in the study it was strangely tidy, with everything stacked and piled in neat heaps. Eric was out too, so Mark supposed he had gone off to bathe again.

Oh, no, he remembered, as one last little flake of onion skin fell off, he couldn't have been doing that all the times he said he had because Tilney said the river was at the other side of the farm. Why ever did Eric make such a mystery about what he did too? And where was he now? Surely he couldn't want to go and see Evangeline before breakfast? What an odd chap he was. But a funny, sort of pathetic one too, what with Evangeline and his super-tough walking boots; it was difficult to know what to think or feel about him. But at any rate, thought Mark, there was one jolly good thing about it all. Everyone was so much involved in work, love letters and problems generally that they had all forgotten he was supposed to be being crammed.

Except by Mrs Tompsett's meals, he thought happily, and as he finished the last well-loaded bit of toast he heard a noise on the brick path outside. Eric, not gone away after all but bustling like the white rabbit, came blinking and flustering into the room.

'Well, we've got your father off to Canterbury all right,' he said, and Mark looked at him in scorn. It was like a tug announcing that it had got off the Queen Mary.

'Your father's a wonderful man, you know.' Well, of course he knew but Mark softened a bit and looked curiously at his tutor. He really was a funny chap, wringing his hands now and bleating in a sort of distressed way, although his large pale eyes were shining with admiration. 'To be able to work with someone with a brain like that; it's such a privilege! These last two days, I can't tell you what an eye-opener they've been to me, Mark ...' and Mark's scorn returned because anyone but a chump would have known how splendid his father was from the beginning.

'But...' Eric was wringing his hands harder than ever, 'The dreadful thing is ... the dreadful thing is that I've lost something,' he went on quickly, '... only a personal thing... a sheet of paper, but it's most important; I must have dropped it. I don't suppose you've seen it anywhere, have you?' and Mark dived his face into his empty mug to hide his flaming cheeks.

'I...' he began, suddenly realising how truly awful it was to take a bit of someone else's letter, and he was just going to fish it out of his pocket and say he had found it when the telephone rang. As Eric flurried off to answer it there was a tap at the window and Mark saw Tilney's head bob upwards and a hand summon him out. Oh, well, he would give the letter back to Eric this evening; it would be less embarrassing that way.

'Well, of course we can read it!' said Tilney scornfully, when they were a couple of fields away and Mark had told her his doubts. 'He dropped it, didn't he? And you can read anything you find dropped on the ground. Think of all those bits that blow out of dustbins. People ought to be more careful if they want to keep their things private. Anyway... don't you want to know about ... you know what?'

Up to that moment Mark hadn't really very much cared but the moment he saw Tilney's pursed-up lips and round, mysterious eyes he found that she was beginning to have her old teasing effect on him again and he did. Memories of yesterday evening came back to him and of how strangely frightening that corner had been; of the worm-eaten hole in the tree and the letters on its trunk, of the smell of tobacco and of rushing away. But there had been something so strangely exhilarating and exciting about the evening too, he remembered being able to run faster that he had ever run before, so that it had seemed more like flying than like ordinary running. He shook his head again.

'Yes,' he said, 'but only if you let me drop the letter afterwards and tell Eric that we know where it is.' He didn't really agree with Tilney's ideas about the rights and wrongs of picking up things at all.

'I think that's worse,' said Tilney, 'but you can if you want to. Now let me see it,' and Mark reluctantly handed over the sheet of paper. He watched her, wondering if she would smile her funny cat smile again, and Tilney bent down her small, spiky nose and unfolded the sheet.

Her hair had swung forward to brush the paper but suddenly it shot back again as she jerked up her head, staring at Mark and not smiling at all.

'This isn't the right one,' she said. 'It's figures and something. You've done it wrong. Look!' and she pushed the sheet angrily into Mark's hands.

As he uncrumpled it he saw some scribbling, a whole lot of

figures scrawled in Eric's large and painstaking hand, that looked like some of the rough notes for his lessons. Then he looked more closely. It couldn't be because it wasn't the sort of sum that he'd ever done, it was much too complicated, with x's and y's and small squiggles like a doctor's prescription and then a whole row of figures with three threes in the middle. His main feeling was one of relief that it wasn't a letter after all and he supposed that old Eric had been doing some sort of homework or other, but why should he have been so agitated about losing it? He screwed the paper up again.

'Well, go on, tell me about your chap then,' he said. 'Whatever there is on the paper, it was the piece that Eric dropped and I did get it, so it's perfectly fair.'

Tilney looked at him, wondering if she could spin things out a little longer, but she waited too long for her purpose. While she was hesitating a sort of delayed action had been going on in Mark's brain. The first time he looked at the figures and squiggles they hadn't meant anything to him, but their imprint must have stayed on his mind all the same for now they began to seem vaguely familiar, like a photograph of someone you had once seen. And as he stopped thinking about them to ask Tilney about her silly sorcerer, his subconscious must have been doing some secret filing for him for suddenly something clicked and the answer shot up.

Three threes, like the 3rd of March, his birthday. He had seen something like that before, quite recently. On another sheet of paper, fluttering about. Then weighted down, under a book, because he had been trying to straighten it. Now he knew where he'd seen that sheet before!

'Well...' began Tilney slowly, as though to give her revelation full weight. 'He...'

But Mark wasn't paying the slightest attention. He had pulled the paper open again and was staring first at it and then at her.

'This was on one of my father's papers,' he said slowly, 'one of the most important ones. Eric's copied it. But why on earth should he, and why should he be wandering about the wood with it, all mixed up with his letter to Evangeline?'

'I don't know!' cried Tilney impatiently. 'Why shouldn't he? Perhaps Evangeline likes maths. Don't you want to hear?'

'Oh, all right, tell me,' said Mark, hardly listening, 'but I still think there's something funny about it. Oh, go on, for goodness' sake tell!' for Tilney's face was beginning to get its shut expression again, and for peace's sake it seemed better to keep her in a good mood. Really, he was getting heartily sick of all this. 'Go on, tell me. What's this old chap like? Has he got a dragon's tail or something?'

'Oh, don't be silly!' said Tilney, important and pleased again. But the moment she tried to start telling him she grew frightened and her voice went tiny. 'I don't even like talking about it,' she said and shivered.

'Well, you see ... I went round the elephant tree,' she said, all in a rush, 'like I always do, and I stretched out to see if the letters on the bark had grown and then my hand came to the hole and I started to feel in it, and I felt ...' she moved nearer to Mark as if for reassurance, 'I felt somebody's hand there! And when I tried to pull mine away this other one grabbed it, and it ... it had a sort of horrid finger, hanging down!'

The effect of her last words was more startling than she could possibly have hoped for. Mark humped up and stared at her wildly.

'A broken finger!' he said. 'But it couldn't be! He's abroad. What did he sound like? Did you see him? Did he say anything to you?'

'Yes, I did,' said Tilney, still almost in a whisper. 'That was more awful still! He pulled me round the tree to look at me and he had dark, treacly sort of eyes and he said, "Go away!" and that I wasn't to come near there again or I'd disturb him. In a horrible, hissing sort of voice, like...'

'Like a kettle,' said Mark. 'I know. It's Dr Barth.' He was now completely convinced. 'But why on earth should he be here? Why...' The questions dripped into his brain one after another, like drops from a tap. What an extraordinary thing! Why didn't his father know, or Eric Clay? Why hadn't Dr Barth come over to see them?

'I think he's staying in the empty cottage at the edge of the wood,' said Tilney still in her small and awe-struck voice, 'they said it was let.' Mark stared at her and all the odd, separate facts began to run together like quicksilver and join up.

Eric Clay, standing by the corner yesterday with that bunch of papers; then Dr Barth coming there and feeling for something in the letter-hole. And Eric had come to them through Dr Barth. Then Mark had a sudden memory of his father's voice, talking to Seb one day and saying that he knew there were one or two other people on the track of his discovery and who were close to getting the answer too. It always happened like that, he said, as though ideas were hanging about in the air and it was just a question of who got them down first.

But it was his father, Max Munday, who had succeeded and had got to be the first person in the world to tell everyone about it in his lecture next week! Unless ... Unless someone copied and stole his ideas and claimed them first. And Eric had been doing just that, Mark realised, horrified, and had been taking them somewhere. To Dr Barth! ... As he thought of Tilney's story Mark suddenly remembered that time in his father's study in Sicily Place and the hand that had been on one of the papers then.

'All those bits of paper that we saw weren't letters to Evangeline,' he said slowly. 'They were my father's secrets. Eric must have pinched them for Dr Barth so that he should be the first person to say about the discovery; so that my father wouldn't be famous after all! It was him all along! Coming into our house and pretending to be a friend of my father's; getting hold of all his ideas and now...'

'Oh, don't be so stupid!' said Tilney, who didn't understand and was getting bored, and Mark suddenly turned on her in a white hot fury.

'It isn't stupid!' He thought of all his father's work, all that thinking, all that reading, and then of someone else getting the credit instead of him; he thought of what his father's face would look like when he knew. And then suddenly, as his feelings grew stronger and stronger, they seemed to turn into a wind. A wind that blew all his muddled thoughts away and scattered them, a wind that had only one idea in it, to get those papers back again before it was too late and stop this thing happening to his father.

It rushed through Mark's veins and filled his heart and head with such strength that he felt he could push down all the trees in the wood to get what he wanted, that he could tear open the elephant tree, branch from branch. As though he was a tunnel quite empty of everything else the thoughts of Tilney and all the silly things they'd been doing, of his piglets and of hoping to impress Seb and Evie, even the longing for his father to think well of him flew away like leaves in a storm. He only wanted one thing and he wanted it with everything that was in him.

Barely conscious of Tilney's startled face left behind him he set off running and as he did so he felt beside him the warm, swift, brush of fur.

'Midway!' he cried, and as they tore down the path towards the monster tree they seemed to rise in the air together, like the pigeons, like the sky-horse, like the greatest of all the beasts in the museum.

'Midway! You've got wings!'

21

'WINGS!' repeated Mark in awe as he saw the great feathered things soaring and shining from Midway's shoulders.

'That or anything else in the world if you want it enough,' said the tiger. 'Come on; you called me the loudest you've ever called and there's no time to waste!' and once again, as Mark put out a hand to touch the shining skin beside him, he had the most extraordinary feeling that some sort of electricity was joining them together. As Midway started off in long, loping bounds, so Mark seemed able to leap along the path too, with the ground skimming away beneath and their thoughts humming to and fro between them like vibrating telegraph wires.

The look-out tree and the next one flicked past them and then suddenly, as they flew round the corner, there was the tangling mass of grey limbs fanning up in front of them and the monster tree in all its vastness rose into the sky. Midway's soft pads, which had seemed to be airborne, slurred on the ground in front of it and then stopped and with the shock of the stopping Mark slid downwards through fur and on to the grass.

'There might be the last lot of notes, the most important ones, still in the tree,' he whispered urgently. 'Eric's been out already!' Oh, if only they might be, so that he could get them before Dr Barth did! From where he and Midway were crouched the great tree trunk hid the path that led off beyond it and Mark started edging round. 'They...'

'Sssh...' Though he had hardly known whether he had been speaking aloud or not, a paw had come over Mark's mouth like a furry pad and as the tiger flattened himself in the grass, limp as a dropped glove, Mark clumsily tried to copy him. As before, long after Midway had picked it up, he heard a faint crackling noise as though someone were making a cautious way towards them through the undergrowth but when he stilled himself down to listen it stopped altogether, till it seemed only to have been a noise in his own ears.

'Some animal, I suppose,' said Midway disapprovingly, as though ashamed to think that anything other than human could make such a noise, and they got up again. Mark walked round the tree, took one nervous look to see that the strange bit of path ahead of it was empty and then looked at the hole. He put his hand out, hesitated for a moment, as he remembered Tilney's story, then looked at Midway's compelling eyes and plunged it in.

With the one bit of his mind that still went back to the staircase monsters and Tilney he half expected that Dr Barth would have put some sort of guardian spitting toad there and he felt gingerly, wondering if he would touch something slimy, or be bitten, but his fingers only met the tindery flaking wood inside. Then ... he plunged deeper. Yes! Paper! He pulled it out triumphantly and rushed back again to the home side of the tree which seemed so much safer.

'There's only one sheet,' he said doubtfully, smoothing it out as he leant against the crouching Midway, using his solid shoulder as a prop. 'I thought there should be more. E.C. – That's Eric's initials, it's funny to put them at the top. No, it isn't notes, it's a letter to Eric.' He read it out.

'"E.C. One page of the last lot missing.
Bring that and any more direct to cottage
and put with others. Must leave at five."

and then that sort of squiggled B. Yes, it is him, I know it.

It's what he writes when he leaves notes in the hall at home.' Mark looked at Midway.

'Tilney said she thought he was staying in a cottage at the edge of the wood. If we go there...' A most unpleasant picture of Dr Barth suddenly came into his mind, but he went on, 'if we can get into it when he's not there, we might be in time to get everything; all the other papers too.'

The tiger nodded and as Mark, nervous of starting, put his fingertips on the fur again, the same tingling electricity sprang up between them. Midway came round the tree and looked down the path ahead of them.

'It may be quite close,' he said. 'We must go carefully. Do as I do,' and he slipped stealthily forward into the undergrowth at the track's edge, blotting himself into the shadows and flicking quickly past the patches of sun as though he were sunlight himself. Mark, trying to put his feet exactly where Midway had placed his, to slip through the tangling brambles in the same liquid way, was at first dismally aware of his human clumsiness and then gradually began to get the hang of it and to feel immensely clever.

This was a wonderful game! To be tracking someone through a forest, to have become like a rippling tiger oneself, to follow without making any noise... He looked ahead. But what was he following? Where was Midway? Mark stopped and then stamped in his blind fury with himself.

He'd forgotten again. Even at a time like this he had let his mind wander off from getting his father's papers. He made all his attention come back and directed it like a torch beam down the path ahead of him. Even if he had to do it without Midway he must get there, even...

'Just in time! But if you make a din like that you'll send up every bird and animal for miles around!' said the striped form that now stood quite plainly ahead of him, 'Then everyone will know that we're coming. Look, there it is!' and Mark, narrowing his eyes to look towards the end of the path, saw a small cottage, much more modern than Watty's, where the trees began to thin. So lightly now that they hardly seemed to touch the ground they crept up towards it and then crouched in the bushes opposite as they stared up.

'It looks empty,' said Mark. 'But . . .' as he managed to push down his fears he felt the electric sparkle again. 'But I'll go and see,' he said firmly. If the papers were really there, if he could still be in time to get them!

'Ssh!' For the second time a paw restrained him and for a moment they both listened. At first Mark was aware again of the oppressive country silence, so heavy that it now seemed certain the cottage must be empty, then he heard the same little crackling noise in the bushes again. As they listened it stopped and he and Midway looked at each other. It must only have been that same small bird or animal as nervous of discovery as they were. The tiger took his paw away and nodded and the two of them, with Mark leading, slipped across the silent sunlight on the path and up to the cottage door.

He shivered and kept his hand on Midway, remembering the unpleasant, steamy atmosphere in Sicily Place, for here again the thick feeling of Dr Barth seemed to be hanging about in musty layers in the room, as dense as the thick plush cloth on the cottage table.

But Mark's eyes only rested on the cloth for a second. He darted forward to the brief-case that lay on it with its flap open. Half-way into this, as though ready to have others added to them, was tucked a thick sheaf of papers, all ready to be sent off somewhere. On top of these was another half sheet with something scrawled on it. Mark picked it up.

'E.C.' it said again at the top, the letters underlined. 'Put missing papers in here. Will take tonight.'

Mark looked at some of the papers beneath. On the top one was a title, the name of his father's own, special subject. 'Broadcast by Dr E. B. Barth,' said the line underneath, and then a date. Tomorrow's! So that was how he was going to announce his father's discoveries and pretend they were his own! Well, he wouldn't be able to now. But as he put down the note for Eric, instead of feeling triumphant because he had spoilt Dr Barth's game, Mark suddenly felt horribly depressed.

So it was really, absolutely true. Eric had been pinching his father's papers. Up till now, even after the first note in the tree, Mark had somehow hoped that it might all have turned out to be a mistake. He wished it hadn't been Eric. A picture came into his mind of his funny neat little house and of the old Ma waving away at the gate, of Eric's bubbling eagerness and his baby blue shirts, of his pale eyes shining with enthusiasm as he listened to Mr Munday. Of him crashing happily through the undergrowth with his rambling friends ... and now ... Oh, it was horrible to find out bad things about someone you knew; it was the most horrible thing in the world!

Mark put his hand back again on Midway's ruff and as they stood there in the frowsy little cottage room together the tiger rubbed his head against Mark's legs and a rough tongue rasped against them. It made him feel better.

Well, it wasn't nice, but it had happened. It would be all right for his father now if he got the papers away before Dr Barth came back. Mark slowly shut down the flap of the brief-case and then thought that he had better go upstairs. There might be some more there and he'd better make a good job of looking while he was here. Picking up the case almost without noticing he had it, Mark, with Midway padding behind him, went up.

There was a tiny landing at the top with three small rooms off it of which only one seemed to be being used. As Mark went into this he looked round for any more odd papers, but the only thing of any interest he could see was a pair of

binoculars on the dressing-table. He couldn't resist picking them up and looking out of the window.

As the glasses wavered unfocused in his hands all he saw at first was a mass of furry greenery, then a tree trunk loomed up at him, looking near enough to hit. The monster tree! Gosh, they must be pretty powerful glasses; he wondered if he could see right into the letter-hole with them? Starting too high in his search for it he then swung the glasses down far too low so that all he could see was small stones and tree roots and ... a pair of feet.

Slowly and reluctantly Mark raised the binoculars again, but this time not up the tree trunk. For the feet had been all too familiar. Clean socks above them, then billowing shorts and a blue shirt. Yes, coming round the tree from the direction of the farm was Eric Clay, his hair ruffled and his expression more worried than ever, his arms hanging loosely and still clutching some papers in one hand.

Mark put the glasses down. At the sight of Eric with his father's notes his anger started rising like mercury in a thermometer. It was horrible and he felt sick.

Eric was so near to the cottage now that Mark could see him just as well without the glasses. As he picked up the brief-case again he saw his tutor look up, evidently towards someone coming along the path from the direction of the village and whom Mark couldn't yet see. As Mark stiffened and watched him with horror Eric shuffled the papers together and held them in his left hand while he searched in his pocket with the other.

For some more, he supposed. Mark could hear the approaching footsteps now and the sound of someone clearing his throat. What could he do? Could he jump there and then from the window? But it was too small and high and by the time he had got down by any other way the papers would have been handed over.

'Eric!' he tried to shout in a voice which started as a crack and then suddenly became a sort of roar. 'Don't do it!' and then as Eric jumped and took a startled look up Mark saw what he had taken from his pocket. It was a lighter and Eric flicked it, once, twice – at the third time it flamed and he put it quickly at the edge of the flimsy papers in his hand.

'Oh, good!' shouted Mark. 'I knew he was all right! Come on, Midway!' and whooping and yelling like a lunatic, he charged down the stairs and out of the front door, just in time to cut between Eric and Dr Barth, who, more loathsome than ever in holiday clothes, in a pale suit that made his sallow face look even yellower, had rushed forward to try to stamp out the burning paper.

22

WAS Midway still there? Not actually, perhaps, but Mark was never really sure for the small woodland path seemed suddenly to be full of anger and dust and people shouting at each other, and the disturbed bars of sunlight might easily have been stripes of tawny fur. But that his strength was with Mark, as it had been in the study at home that time, and seemed to be more and more, was quite certain. Full of it and knowing quite clearly what he should do, Mark swung something at Dr Barth to knock him out of the way and grabbed hold of Eric, pulling him into the undergrowth and away between the twisting tree trunks.

For a while footsteps came crashing after them, but then they heard them grow slower and more uncertain till at last they stopped altogether. Mark led on for a while until he felt safe, then stopped, and, except for the small occasional rustle of a bird or animal and the beating of his own heart, the wood seemed to have grown quite still.

'I . . .' began Eric, as soon as he had got any breath.

This was dreadful and Mark squirmed; he didn't want to talk about what had happened.

'It doesn't matter,' he said quickly and for a moment Midway was quite definitely by his side again.

'What are we going to do?' he asked Eric, plumping his things down in the grass. The awful thing was that it suddenly seemed to be him that had to decide and he felt very odd, as though he had suddenly grown about three years older.

'Dr Barth's going up to London tonight; he's got his broadcast tomorrow,' said Eric miserably and all the fatness and bounciness seemed to have sagged out of him and left him like an empty sock. 'Even without those last papers there's still quite a lot that ... that I got for him. Enough to spoil your father's lecture. Oh, why did I do it, Mark?' He was wringing his hands again and bleating. 'It was because...'

'Oh, shut up,' said Mark; he really couldn't bear this, and besides he wanted to think.

'I suppose it's like one of those newspaper competition things,' he said. 'If two people both say nearly the same thing it's the first one to say it who wins?'

He was plucking at a tuft of grass beside him as he spoke and then quite suddenly he stared down and started to laugh. Then he fished up the something that had been lying there, half hidden in the long grass beside him.

'I am a clot! Of course Dr Barth can't say it or broadcast it or whatever he was going to do, because I've still got his brief-case with all the papers in!' He threw it up in the air and caught it again in his relief.

'Oh, do be careful, Mark! said Eric, looking anxiously round. 'He'll be after us as soon as he discovers it's gone.'

'Yes, we'll have to get on.' Mark stood up, swinging the brief-case and then frowned as he looked down at it. He suddenly knew that he didn't want to take the beastly thing back to the oast-house because then his father would have to know about Eric and there would have to be the most horrible explanations; if the things in here were only copies it wouldn't matter if no one ever saw them again. He just wanted to hide it, to get rid of it; but where? He thought of the wood, then of Midway's look-out tree and of all the fire-break paths that they had seen from it and none of them seemed completely safe from Dr Barth. He thought of Watty's cottage, the pigs, the straw of the sty...

'I know!' he said. 'Come on!' Blanche would be a match for the doctor if he tracked it down.

He looked round again. But how did they get to Watty's cottage from here? They had come much farther away from the path than he had realised and the criss-crossing branches closed round them on all sides like a grille. He didn't even know which direction they had come from now and one look at the still hand-wringing Eric told him that for the moment all his tutor's rambler instincts had deserted him and that he would be about as much use as a sick headache.

If they went the wrong way they might run straight into Dr Barth again; he might just be waiting for them now, keeping very quiet. But was he keeping so quiet? Mark's ears, which seemed to have grown much more alert, picked out a faint rustling like that he had heard earlier, a rustling that grew into a brushing and then into a crackle of twigs, finally into footsteps coming towards them through the trees. He clasped the brief-case tight with both hands behind him, ready to swing it again if necessary, ready to run.

'What on earth are you doing?' asked Tilney, as she stepped out from under a branch and then shook some twigs from her hair as she stared at them both, 'I could hear you talking miles away.'

But this was no time for answering questions. 'Is that the way back to Watty's?' asked Mark, pointing behind her, and, opening her eyes wide for a moment in surprise, Tilney gave way to his new-found authority. She nodded and led them back through the trees.

They had not been going for more than a few minutes and had thankfully come out on to the path by the look-out tree when Tilney stopped and sniffed.

'Oh, come on!' said Mark, but this time it didn't work.

Tilney only sniffed deeper. 'There's something burning,' she said, and put up a warning finger. 'Listen. Smell.'

It seemed funny to listen for a smell but Mark strained his ears and sure enough he did seem to need both senses. After a second or two's deep breathing he could detect a smoky smell above that of the sun-warmed pine needles, and then, at about the third breath, it seemed all to be smoke and hardly any pine. And then he heard the noise.

Very faint and far off it was at first, a delicate crackling, as though someone were tiptoeing after them through the brambles in tennis shoes.

'It's Dr Barth.'

'No, it's not,' said Tilney firmly. 'Don't be silly. It's a fire and that's the brambles and bracken catching; I've heard it before. I'm going up to see,' and as the distant crackling seemed to burst out afresh in a series of sharp little explosions Mark and Eric saw her short skirt shoot suddenly up the look-out tree till it was only a small blue patch among the upper branches.

She was back again almost instantly, so quickly that she seemed to have dropped down on a rope like a spider, her eyes wide with alarm.

'The wood's caught!' she said. 'It's from where you burnt the letters!' she said accusingly to Eric, 'and it's blowing right down the middle path. It'll get to our fields and hay stacks!'

So she'd been following him and watching all the time! It must have been her rustling that he and Midway heard, but there was no time to worry about that now.

'And to Watty's,' said Mark, 'and my pigs!' In a confused, distressed picture he saw their thin little pink skins with the flames coming near them and their cheerful eyes gone all frightened as they smelt the smoke.

'I'm going back to tell Bill'n'Harry,' panted Tilney, pointing, breathless from her climb, 'they're out there in the five-acre, I saw them,' and then with her hand on her side, because she'd got a stitch from going up and down so fast, she doubled herself up to try and get her breath.

'I'll go to Watty's,' Mark and Tilney both looked at Eric, who was once again crumpling and wringing his hands.

'And me a rambler!' he said. 'To set fire to the woodland!' It seemed as though his cup of shame and misery were full.

Then he stopped wringing his hands and clenched them.

'I'll go back to the cottage and telephone the fire-brigade,' he said.

'Straight back to Dr Barth?' asked Mark incredulously. 'He'll murder you!'

'I know,' said Eric with a pathetic and curious dignity, 'but he'll let me telephone first.'

Mark gave him a quick glance of appreciation and then as Tilney, now fully replenished with breath, shot off like a pea from a catapult towards the farm, he rushed off too, brief-case swinging from one hand, down the side track towards Watty's clearing. He didn't stop until he was outside her door and hammering on its grey bleached wood, the case still dangling from one hand.

'What's that you say?' Watty's slow footsteps had brought her to the door at last. 'Fire?' She jerked back her head for a moment to smell and listen as Tilney had done, then she and Mark looked at each other briefly. The crackling had grown much louder and underneath it, like a crowd at a distant football match, there was a steady, ever-increasing roar.

'The hose,' she said, 'I reckon the fire should go round here, the last one did, we're in a clearing. But there's the straw by the pigsties and a spark might start that off. Look, you take this rake and get it up.'

She pointed and as Mark took up the hay rake she disappeared into an out-building and came out again tugging a serpent-like coil.

As they neared Blanche Mark could hear the noise of grunting and the exciting small squeals beneath it but as he quickly dropped the brief-case over he daren't even take time to look over the low wall of the sty just yet.

He raked away like mad, scratching the blown and scattered straw from the space between the sty and where the wood started, leaving only bare earth on which sparks couldn't catch. The wind that blew from between the trees was growing warmer every minute, as though some giant heater had been turned on.

As Mark got the last of the straw heaped up and threw it in armfuls over the wall of an empty pig-sty, it suddenly seemed to be raining, but he found it was only Watty, directing the hose's spray to damp down the earth. Then at last, half-drenched himself, but thankful for the coolness, Mark looked over the wall at his last night's friends. It was almost incredible, instead of the puny creatures they had been they were now three very proper, real, live, growing pigs; warm and pink and healthy. The miraculous feeling of last night came back to him and the wonderful thought that perhaps he could do the same with other animals; spend his whole life doing it. Oh, he must find out the right things to do, ask Mr Castle, get books about it to read! As the thought of his new future flickered briefly in front of him, as full of things that he really wanted to do as the Christmas holidays were with parties, he leant thankfully over to touch one of the piglets. It let go of the now placid Blanche and looked round at him with a rakish eye.

'Small!' cried Mark, recognising it with delight, and he could have sworn it winked back at him.

'Should be all right,' grunted Watty, 'if the water holds out and the Brigade comes quickly. There's a pond in the wood they'll use. The hoppers might help.' She looked at Mark. 'One way and another, you seem connected with these pigs,' she said, 'I think we'll have to keep them.'

Keep Cowslick and Squealer and Small! She was just grinning at his delight when they heard the blessed sound of the sirens in the distance, wailing through the roar that now sounded like a stormy sea.

'Did you say the fire started on the far side of the wood?' Watty asked Mark. She wetted a finger and held it up. 'The wind's north-west,' she said, 'so with any luck it won't come this way,' but as she stood there with the nozzle of the hose in her hand and her short hair full of blown bits of straw, she looked worried.

'It'll drive straight for Tompsett's haystacks,' she said. 'Unless . . .'

'Tilney's gone to tell them.' As Mark leant over and nearly capsized in a vain attempt to scratch all the three piglets at once, so fierce with protection for them, ready to pick them up and bolt with them through the flaming forest if need arose, they heard a siren again, from the other direction.

'That's all right then,' said Watty. 'That'll be the Fincham lot. Look, Mark, you run up to the attic for me and see whether they're getting the fire under control. Straight up the stairs, little bedroom on the right; ladder up through the trap-door. All right,' she said, as he hesitated for a moment, 'I'll look after 'em for you,' and she gave him another dusty and grimy grin as he let go of Squealer, straightened and dashed off for the cottage.

He pushed open the front door and ran down the dark passage along which Watty usually came so slowly; the carpet on the stairs was so old and loose that he tripped and fell up them twice before he got to the top.

'Bedroom on the right.' It looked more like a junk room than a bedroom but as he pushed through the dusty and piled up old furniture Mark had eyes only for the ladder up to the attic. He climbed its few steps, found that he had to push open the trap-door with his head and then was up in the sunny, dusty, sloping room. There was a small window high in one wall and he had to pull up an old trunk to stand on before he could look out.

There was such a wide sweep of view that at first it was like when he had looked through the unfocused binoculars and he didn't know where to start. Below came the edge of the wood they were in, then the fields of stubble, running away towards the oast-house and the farm, where he could see little men scurrying about like ants, carrying a great hose from the pond and the engine that was standing beside it, towards the hay-stacks.

There a group of farm men were running to and fro as well, some raking round the stacks as he had done round the pigsties, some waiting with fire brooms to beat out the flames as they might appear. Flittering about among them, like a blue butterfly, he saw Tilney.

Mark moved to the far corner of the trunk to look back and see what was happening in the wood. On their side of the track it still seemed to be all right for the leaves were green and only blowing gently in the breeze. But beyond it, on the far side, the air just above the brown tops of the trees was full of steaming smoke as though someone were boiling a giant kettle. Suddenly, to Mark's horror, he saw a branch break and fall with a dreadful cracking noise, tearing a hole in the surrounding leaves as it plunged downwards. And then he saw the actual fire, orange and sinister, licking its way out and across an open patch of bracken, sending a dark coil of smoke upwards.

He looked anxiously back at the fire-engine. Men were lined up all along the fringe of the wood by the hay-stack now. Then, from his superior vantage point in the high-up window, he suddenly saw something that they couldn't. From the edge of the wood, by the gate where he had first come in with Tilney, a small trail of fire had escaped and crept out. At first it only seemed to be picking its way cautiously but the moment it got out of the shelter of the wood and the breeze caught it sideways it dashed on ahead, crossing the field behind the busy firemen's backs at an angle away from the farm buildings and driving straight towards the oast.

From here Mark could see the house quite clearly, the garden and rose bushes, the windows up above, peacefully open in the sun. What had he left there, wondered Mark anxiously, looking at his own window. His camera, his ... But suddenly his heart gave a great lurch as he looked at the window on the other side. His father's papers were there! Stacked quite near the window! He turned and jumped down from the trunk. No one at the farm even knew what important things were in that room. Visitors' clothes, they'd think, and holiday books and things, none of them in the least important compared with animals and barns and hay.

Then suddenly he remembered something else. But of course! He'd got duplicates of all those papers now, in the brief-case. He must get it quickly and put it somewhere safe.

As swiftly as Tilney had come down the tree he was down the attic ladder and the stairs and along the stone passage again. From the front door he saw Watty's strange and stocky figure on guard by the sties, then, as he looked, he saw her suddenly bend over to deal with something inside.

'No! Blanche; leave it!' he heard her shout.

His piglets! Had she gone wild again? He ran over quickly to join Watty.

'Mark! Were these anything important?'

He stared for one second at the trampled leather and the confetti of chewed up paper and that was enough. He'd got to get to the oast now, there wasn't any choice.

'The fire's driving towards the oast where my father's things are; I've got to go! Oh, please look after the piglets!' and Watty, accepting without question that he must go, nodded.

Mark realised that it wasn't any good going back to the path through the middle of the wood because the smoke there was as thick now as a London fog, he must break his way through the undergrowth to the edge of the wood. Fighting the maddening brambles that tore at his clothes and undid his shoelaces, pushing away the whipping twigs that snapped back and stung across his face he managed at last to

plunge through a clump of nettles, hardly noticing their stinging, and came out panting on the other side, at the edge of the open field.

He started running across the green stubble, taking a slanting path towards the oast-house. After a while it grew brown under his feet, then black, and then he stopped in dismay. He had been running in one line and the tongues of fire he had seen from the wood had been coming in another line verging towards it. Now they had nearly met. To get near enough to make the firemen see and hear him he had to go over the smouldering part of the stubble; through the smoke.

Mark stopped for a second, all alone in the middle of the burning field and sniffed the bitter smell; then, as the smoke got into his lungs and he coughed panic rooted him there. This was what animals must feel like when they smelt fire, he thought, this was what Cowslick and Squealer and Small would feel, this was what Midway ...

But Midway couldn't be frightened! The certain thought came rushing into him. There was no power on earth could frighten him! He could have anything he wanted, he had said, wings like the wind or muscles hard as bronze if Mark wanted it hard enough, and oh how he wanted them now! He must get to the firemen and make them save the oast-house!

He looked round desperately, beseechingly, and then suddenly not springing up from anywhere else in the field, not from beside Mark or behind him but from right out of the very middle of him, more glorious and more splendid than ever, Midway was there.

23

IT was only about half an hour later, though it seemed to Mark like years and centuries, that he came down the oast-house stairs. He was so tired that he felt as though he had to pull each leg out of treacle at every step but he felt happy as he leant, unnoticed, against the jamb of the door into the garden.

Outside, with his back to Mark, was the solid comfort of his father's large figure. He had evidently just got back and was questioning one of the firemen.

'Yes, all the building's all right, sir,' he heard the man say as he came out of the door and into the garden himself, 'but we'd never have spotted that the fire was heading this way so early if it hadn't been for that young fellow of yours! He came dashing out of the wood to warn us and right across the stubble that had caught like – just like a tiger! And nipped up inside, to get something precious, he said, before any of us could stop him . . . 'course we'd got the hoses on it by then so we knew he couldn't come to any harm.'

'The hoses?' Mark heard his father say anxiously as he moved slightly towards him, looking at all the mass of chattering people and paraphernalia cluttering the garden behind. He had to hop over a twining loop of hose and this was difficult because he seemed to have grown a blister on the hopping part of his foot.

'Yes, we gave the oast a rare good drenching, I'm afraid, I don't know how you'll find your things inside! Still, I dare say it's better having a few things wet than all burnt away.'

'Wet?' Max Munday stared at him. 'Oh, lord, all my things were by the window and I left it open!' He turned towards the oast-house door, but Mark tugged at his hand.

'It's all right, Father,' he said, 'I got them shut in time. Only just though. Gosh! That water didn't half make a noise on the windows! Like a thunderstorm!' It had been one of the most welcoming noises he had ever heard, that solid shut glass taking the force of the water.

'Mark!' His father looked down and held the tugging hand tightly. 'You remembered my papers! I thought it was something of yours that you had gone to get! But are you all right? That's much more important.'

More important! Happy and speechless, Mark grinned and nodded his head. Then he looked round because he didn't want to waste any minute of this; it wasn't every day that you found yourself right on the scene of a fire. Although the blaze at the farm edge of the wood had been beaten down and was cringing away now to the faintest of hissing splutters, the hoses, held by splendid firemen, were still jetting out silver ropes. Mark had just anxiously asked about Watty's cottage and heard that it was quite all right when he saw the village taxi drive up and stop at the far gate and then the familiar figures of Seb and Evie drag out their baggage and run up under a sort of watery triumphal arch.

Trust them! They always did manage to arrive anywhere in the middle of excitement, thought Mark, his old habit of envy returning, then he suddenly remembered that he himself was in the very heart of the excitement and had been there for hours and he grinned.

'Hallo!' he said and was looking at Evie's water-spangled hair to see from its redness whether she was still languishing for Alexander or had got a good new one, when he saw her look quickly over towards the fire-engine, then stop transfixed and stare.

'Here we go!' said Seb to Mark. 'There wasn't anyone in France, not the whole time we were there, thank heaven. She's been comparatively sane. Have you been in all this from the beginning?' and as Evie gazed, lost, at the tallest and most splendidly helmeted fireman, so Seb, the lordly Seb, looked down at Mark in envy. Mark's cup was full.

'Hallo, Seb; nice to see you. Mark's just saved all my things from the fire, what do you think of that? I've got to take them up for the lecture tomorrow so I'd have been properly dished if he hadn't.' He put a hand on Mark's shoulder again.

Mark found that the unaccustomed atmosphere of approval was almost too much and wanted to cast some of it on to somebody else.

'It was Tilney who got back here first with the message about the fire,' he said as he saw her. She came towards them, eyeing Evie with interest but otherwise as unruffled as ever.

'Yes, she did that,' said Bert'n'Harry, who seemed always to move and speak as one man. 'We wouldn't have got the Brigade here in time else.'

'And somebody rang from Puckshorn way too, to get the other Brigade,' said another of the men. 'That saved a lot of the woodland; I hear they got it under control quite soon.'

Goodness, thought Mark, he had forgotten about old Eric! Where was he now, he wondered, feeling responsible for him in an odd sort of way, and what had Dr Barth done to him? And then suddenly, among all the bustle, Eric was there, a changed figure, no longer apologetic but flourishing a fire broom heroically and leading a squad of hoppers. Among them, of all extraordinary things on this extraordinary day, was Jamie, beaming and even browner than usual, and three of his magnificent uncles to whom he introduced Mark with pride. Everyone seemed to have heard of Mark's exploit and they nearly lifted him off the ground with their vast handshakes, promising him free boats, free coconut shies, free giant dippers, till he had visions of living free at fairs for the rest of his life.

Evie, who was still gazing at her fireman, and now heard him describing Mark's epic dash across the field, looked at her brother with new eyes and a new admiration.

'He's bald as an egg underneath the helmet!' whispered Tilney from beside Mark. 'D'you think she'll still like him when she sees?' and she flashed him her wrinkled smile.

'Never seen anyone cover the ground so fast ...' the hero was saying, just about to take off his helmet and mop his brow, but Mark didn't manage to see Evie's reaction because then Seb too, talking in the familiar way that Mark had always dreamt he might, started asking him what it had felt like, and did Mark think ...

Did Mark think! Before, it had never seemed to occur to anyone that Mark could think and he was just basking in this new pleasure when Mrs Tompsett appeared in the doorway of the farm, suggesting that they should all go in. As they did so another thought started tugging at Mark's mind. It was something even better than all these goodly things that were happening to him, something more specially his and that was somehow the cause of it all. Was it this business of knowing about his future and wanting to be a vet? As they went through the door and into the living-room he started to tell Seb all about it, and about Cowslick and Squealer and Small, with bubbling enthusiasm, but still he knew that this wasn't quite all; there was another, even better thing, behind.

They were inside now and Mrs Tompsett had lit an enormous fire to get everything dry. As everyone ate, drank and talked all round it, full of thankfulness for their escape, it seemed strange to Mark that anyone should ever be pleased to see a fire again, even a tame one.

But they were, though, and in happy sort of blur himself, his conversation with Seb tailing off, but without it mattering, Mark stared lazily at the leaping flames, watching their orange turn to yellow, the black twigs snapping and melting, white ash ... white stripes ... white ...

'Oh, Midway!' he breathed and now he knew. He knew why all these good things had happened to him so that he was sitting here quite at ease in the middle of his family, not worrying about being as clever as Seb or as spoilt as the twins were but just happy to be himself. He knew why he was able to talk easily again to his father and join in the jokes and chaff that were going on, without feeling stupid; he knew why he now had something he wanted to do that was specially his and not copied from anybody else; that away in the wood Cowslick, Squealer and Small were waiting for him. It was all because Midway had come.

'Oh, Midway!' he said again inside him, because he knew now that none of the others could see what he saw, and then, as he looked, used as he was to the splendours of Midway, he was amazed. Above the fire the great beast grew till he stretched up to touch the ceiling and shone till every silken, quivering hair was like a separate thread of gold. His stripes were like rays of sunset and his eyes shone like the sea at noonday, glowing with all the lively interest, all the wisdom, all the kindness and all the pride in the world.

As a log dropped and a taller flame flared, wings flamed out from the tiger's shoulders too; wings that were copper and gold like the beasts in the museum. As Mark gazed on in wonder, even Midway's tiger face changed till he seemed to become first human and then like one after another of those same beasts and then suddenly he was his own right size again and his own self, just Midway, Mark's Midway, his own special person and tiger; his friend.

Mark felt very strange now for he alone of all the people there seemed to be in two worlds at once. Like the solid logs in the hearth he was aware of all the ordinary people sitting round and was able to listen to their talk, but above them, flaring up like the flames and the light of the fire, he and he alone was aware of Midway, his green eyes bright with the promise of adventure and warm with affection, glittering with the windy starlight of far-off places and yet glowing with the homely friendliness of here and now.

Oh, he would stay with his tiger always, thought Mark, not bother about anyone else at all, but then he heard his father saying something to him across the fire and his attention was drawn back into the ordinary world again. It was about Dr Barth and how Mr Munday had a letter from him that morning saying he was leaving Sicily Place.

'Without any notice and without a word of thanks ... I've been hearing some rather odd things about him too. It doesn't even seem at all certain that he was a doctor. You never liked him, did you, Mark? Well, it looks as if we'll have to pay more attention to your hunches after this! But I mustn't forget to listen to that broadcast of his this evening.'

'If he gives it!' thought Mark happily to himself and then he looked back to Midway again.

'I'll remember you always now,' he vowed, 'I know I shall. And stay with you.'

But as Seb shouted something to him and then Evie joined in, and his father, all making some silly family joke, the pull was too strong for Mark and he had to shout something back across the fire. As the conversation changed and drifted away from him again he looked back and up at his friend.

Glorious and golden but somehow less solid now, the great animal was still flickering up towards the ceiling as though he were made only of light and fire. His eyes still shone as he looked at Mark, but he shook his head.

'You can't stay with me,' he said. 'At least, not outside, that is, and soon you won't want to, anyway,' and as Mark heard the others making plans for tomorrow and wanted to join in with them, he sadly knew this was true.

'I came because you specially needed and called for me; I'll come again if ...'

Oh, what was it he said? It was so difficult to hear him now! Who was it that had been talking to him? Mark was growing so sleepy but suddenly he shook himself awake. As one specially bright flame shot upwards Mark's mind shot up too in a flame of thankfulness and longing.

'Oh, Midway, dear Midway; don't go!' he cried, but he knew that he couldn't stop it, now Midway was hardly there at all. But he had said that he would come again! 'Where shall I find you?' he cried.

'Don't you know yet?' whispered the tiger. 'Haven't you realised? Don't you remember where I came from when you ran across the field?'

Mark's thoughts flickered back. He remembered that last desperate dash of speed and the strength that had suddenly come like the wind from ...

'From inside me!' he cried. 'Midway! Then you are always ...'

But why was he shouting silently inside himself as a flame shot up the chimney, why did it seem to be laughing at him as it rustled? Why did it seem to be saying something to him that he could hardly hear, '... keep me strong, keep me shining ... keep me bright ...'

Honestly, talking to flames! He must be either asleep or off his rocker, thought Mark, but as the door opened and Eric Clay came in with Professor Worsley the sudden draught of cold air woke him up completely again. Introductions were made all round and the story of the fire and the rescue of the papers retold; the professor looked at Mark with admiration and held out his hand.

'So this is the one who saved them! I expect this is your son Sebastian that you've told me so much about?' he asked Mr Munday.

'Oh, no,' said Max Munday easily, in his old, glorious voice of long ago, 'this is Mark, my middle son.'